# ΘΕΛΗΜΑ

## THE HOLY BOOKS
## OF THELEMA

# O.T.O.

𝕴𝖘𝖘𝖚𝖊𝖉 𝖇𝖞 𝕺𝖗𝖉𝖊𝖗:

CALIPH
X° O.T.O.
UNITED STATES OF AMERICA
REX SUMMUS SANCTISSIMUS

THE EQUINOX VOLUME THREE NUMBER NINE

# ΘΕΛΗΜΑ

# THE HOLY BOOKS OF THELEMA

WEISERBOOKS
Boston, MA/York Beach, ME

First published in 1983 by
Red Wheel/Weiser, LLC
P. O. Box 612
York Beach, ME 03910-0612

First paper edition, 1988

07  06  05  04  03  02  01
10  9  8  7  6

Library of Congress Catalog Card Number: 82-50829

ISBN 0-87728-686-8
ISSN 1050-2904
BJ

*Acknowledgements*
O.T.O wishes to thank Mr. G.J. Yorke, Mr D. Montagu, and The Humanities
Research Center at the Universite of Texas at Austin for research assistance and
source materials.

PRINTED IN THE UNITED STATES OF AMERICA

The paper used in this publication meets the minimum requirements of the
American National Standard for Information Sciences—Permanence of Paper for
Printed Library Materials Z39.48-1992(R1997).

# TABLE OF CONTENTS

# PREFACE

*Do what thou wilt shall be the whole of the Law.*

THE HOLY BOOKS OF THELEMA are the chief legacy of their scribe, Aleister Crowley (1875–1947 E.V.). Their principal value to us, his heirs, lies not in their considerable literary merit, but rather in the insight and illumination these books yield on each reading. Written, as they were, on the most exalted planes of spiritual experience, they have a way of unfolding within the reader, of not only retaining, but increasing their relevance. Since these works were written *through* Crowley, they cannot be classed with those books of magical and mystical instruction consciously written *by* Crowley. They afford far more than information or instruction— they give access to the source of the scribe's genius, and can awaken, as if by sympathetic resonance, promptings toward similar experiences in the receptive reader.

The most important *liber* (or book) is the founding document of Thelema: *Liber AL Vel Legis Sub Figurâ CCXX*. Originally titled *Liber L*, it was later retitled *Liber AL* (also pronounced *el*), and is often called *Liber Legis*, or *The Book of the Law*. The reception of this book in Cairo, Egypt, signalled the expiration of the Æon of Osiris, and inaugurated the new Æon of Horus; thus 1904 E.V. (*Era Vulgaris*, or common era) is year 0 of the Thelemic calendar.

The three chapters of *Liber Legis* were literally dictated to Crowley, during three one-hour sessions, from noon to 1 P.M. on April 8, 9 and 10, 1904 E.V. The entity giving dictation was a « præter-human intelligence » called Aiwaz, or Aiwass, a being demonstrating knowledge and prescience beyond anything hitherto associated with human faculties. Crowley describes this messenger, and the circumstances surrounding the dictation of the book, in the following excerpt from his writings:

> The Voice of Aiwass came apparently from over my left shoulder, from the furthest corner of the room. [...] The voice was passionately poured, as if Aiwass were alert about the

time-limit. [ ... ] I had a strong impression that the speaker
was actually in the corner where he seemed to be, in a body of
«fine matter,» transparent as a veil of gauze, or a cloud of
incense-smoke.  He seemed to be a tall, dark man in his
thirties, well-knit, active and strong, with the face of a savage
king, and eyes veiled lest their gaze should destroy what they
saw.  The dress was not Arab; it suggested Assyria or Persia,
but very vaguely.  I took little note of it, for to me at that time
Aiwass was an «angel» such as I had often seen in visions, a
being purely astral.[1]

Crowley later recognized Aiwass as his Holy Guardian Angel, and
came to accept the mantle of Thelemic prophet of the Æon of Horus
thrust upon him by his reception of *Liber Legis*.  Although the book
abounds in specific references to the scribe and prophet in his
now-historical rôle of The Beast 666, it is nevertheless the most
influential of the Holy Books, with the greatest general relevance to
humanity.

*The Book of the Law* was also the origin of the technical class (Class
«A») to which these Holy Books belong.  Chapter I, verse 36, states
that the scribe «shall not in one letter change this book; but lest there
be folly, he shall comment thereupon by the wisdom of Ra-Hoor-
Khu-it.»  Crowley accordingly produced several important commentaries to *Liber Legis*, but only one that he regarded as definitely
inspired—the Comment he received in 1925 E.V., as predicted by
*Liber Legis*:

But the work of the comment?  That is easy; and Hadit burning
in thy heart shall make swift and secure thy pen.[2]

Crowley considered *The Comment* (page 196 of the present volume)
«the really inspired message, cutting as it does all the difficulties with
a single keen stroke.»[3]  This refers to the commentators that would
otherwise revise and distort the message of *Liber Legis* to their own
ends, forming «schools of interpretation» with the conformist
pressures and tendencies to schism that inevitably follow.  *The
Comment* warns against the dissemination of personal interpretations of

---

[1] Crowley, *The Equinox of the Gods* (London: O.T.O., 1936), pp. 117–118.
[2] *Liber Legis* III:40.  See page 125 *infra*.
[3] Crowley, *The Equinox of the Gods*, p. 126n.

the book, thus establishing a scriptural tradition resistant to the revisionism that plagued previous religions and mystery schools. Yet it places supreme emphasis upon individual freedom of interpretation: «All questions of the Law are to be decided only by appeal to my writings, each for himself.» As applied, this creates a climate of freedom without parallel in religious history.

In many ways *Liber Legis* edits itself, giving explicit and detailed instructions to the scribe. These instructions, reviewed below, shed light on the dynamic interaction between scribe and book.

*Liber Legis* places great emphasis upon the importance of preserving the book intact for future generations: «Change not as much as the style of a letter; for behold! thou, o prophet, shalt not behold all these mysteries hidden therein.»[4] Crowley writes of this:

> This injunction was most necessary, for had I been left to myself, I should have wanted to edit the Book ruthlessly. I find in it what I consider faults of style, and even of grammar; much of the matter was at the time of writing most antipathetic. But the Book proved itself greater than the scribe; again and again have the «mistakes» proved themselves to be devices for transmitting a Wisdom beyond the scope of ordinary language.[5]

Another such instruction insists upon «a reproduction of this ink and paper for ever—for in it is the word secret & not only in the English».[6] *Liber Legis* even stipulates that the manuscript be included in foreign-language translations, «for in the chance shape of the letters and their position to one another: in these are mysteries that no Beast shall divine.»[7] In the present volume, the manuscript (technically titled *Liber XXXI*)[8] is reproduced at 56% original size immediately following the typeset text of *Liber CCXX*. Placing *Liber XXXI* after *Liber CCXX* disregards the numerical order (by book

---

[4] *Liber Legis* I:54. See page 111 *infra*.

[5] Crowley, commentary to *Liber Legis* I:54. For bibliographic references to the several editions of the commentaries see Appendix C *infra*.

[6] *Liber Legis* III:39. See page 125 *infra*.

[7] *Liber Legis* III:47. See page 126 *infra*.

[8] Not to be confused with a related book with the same title: *Liber XXXI*, by Frater Achad (Charles Stansfeld Jones) (San Francisco: Level Press, 1974); also *Sothis* I(3) (St. Albans, U.K., 1974), pp. 75–102.

number) otherwise observed in this edition, but facilitates comparison of the text and manuscript.

An important change made by Crowley when editing *Liber CCXX* was his numbering of the verses in Chapter I, which are unnumbered in manuscript. Since *Liber CCXX* derives its title from its total of 220 verses, this title clearly cannot apply to the manuscript. A few recent editions of *Liber Legis* have appeared which follow the MS., *Liber XXXI*, more literally in some respects than does *Liber CCXX*. Technically, such editions are not *Liber CCXX*, but rather attempts to produce a typeset version of *Liber XXXI*.

Finally, a close comparison of the text and manuscript will show variant punctuation. This was anticipated and approved by *Liber Legis*: « The stops as thou wilt; the letters? change them not in style or value! »[9] Thus, the changes in the « stops » introduced by Crowley in preparing *Liber CCXX* from *Liber XXXI* are in accordance with the book's instructions.

Accordingly, each of the above-described prescriptions for publication have been observed in preparing *Liber CCXX* for this edition. The most recent authorized publication of *Liber Legis* has been used: that published by the O.T.O. in 1938 E.V. In recent reprintings (Weiser, 1976, 1981) four typographical errors were corrected by the O.T.O., after verification in earlier authorized editions and the MS.

Having reviewed the means by which *Liber CCXX* was prepared from the manuscript, *Liber XXXI*, it is appropriate here to examine the manuscript itself. In *The Equinox of the Gods* Crowley gives an explanatory list of the departures in *Liber XXXI* from what was dictated during the reception of *Liber Legis*:

> A. On page 6 [of the MS.] Aiwaz instructs me to « write this (what he had just said) in whiter words, » for my mind rebelled at His phrase. He added at once « But go forth on, » *i.e.*, with His utterance, leaving the emendation until later.
>
> B. On page 19 I failed to hear a sentence, and (later on) the Scarlet Woman, invoking Aiwass, wrote in the missing

---

[9] *Liber Legis* II:54. See page 118 *infra*.

words. (How? She was not in the room at the time, and
heard nothing.)

C. Page 20 of Cap. III, I got a phrase indistinctly, and she put
it in, as for «B.»

D. The versified paraphrase of the hieroglyphs on the Stèle
being ready, Aiwaz allowed me to insert these later, so as to
save time.

These four apart, the MS. is exactly as it was written on those
three days.[10]

The stèle (or stela) referred to in §D above is a funerary
monument of Ankh-f-n-khonsu, a Theban priest of Month (or
Mentu) who flourished (according to modern scholarship) *circa* 725
B.C.E., in Egypt's 25th Dynasty.[11] It figured largely in the events
leading up to the reception of *Liber Legis*, as did the Scarlet Woman,
Crowley's wife Rose. It was her discovery of the Stèle in Cairo's
Boulaq Museum that (in Crowley's words) «led to the creation of the
ritual by which Aiwass, the author of *Liber L* [*Liber AL Vel Legis*],
was invoked.»[12]

It is referred to as the Stèle of Revealing in *Liber Legis*, and
according to Crowley, indicates «a certain continuity or identity of
myself with Ankh-f-n-khonsu, whose Stèle is the Link with Antiquity
of this Revelation.»[13] Crowley's comment is of interest when
considering the observations of the Egyptologist Abd el Hamid
Zayed, who gave the Stèle its first publication in the archæological
literature, in 1968 E.V.:

> The back of the stela is occupied by eleven horizontal lines of
> inscription, the first part of which is a version of [*The Book of
> the Dead*], chap. 30. This chapter was usually engraved upon a
> large scarab. It is very unusual to find it inscribed upon a stela.

---

[10] Crowley, *The Equinox of the Gods*, p. 119. Crowley refers to the page numbers
of the MS. itself. For the page referred to in §A, see *Liber XXXI*, p. 136 *infra*.
For §B see p. 149, for §C see p. 194, and for §D see pp. 132 and 184.

[11] R.A. Kitchen, *The Third Intermediate Period in Egypt* (Warminster, U.K.: Aris
& Phillips, 1973), §§190 and 191. See also P. Munro, «Die spätägyptischen
Totenstelen,» *Ägyptologische Forschungen* XXV, 1973, *passim*.

[12] Crowley, note to M. Brugsch Bey (attrib.), «The Stèle, translation and other matters
pertaining to Liber Legis,» Appendix A *infra*.

[13] Crowley, commentary to *Liber Legis* I:5.

The second half of the inscription is part of [*The Book of the Dead*], chap. 2 and, in the Theban Recension, it was entitled: «The chapter of coming forth by day and living after death». *Its object was to allow the astral form of the deceased to revisit the earth at will.*[14] [*emphasis added*]

Certain other observations by Zayed are of interest. He notes that painted wooden stelæ are uncommon, since stelæ were usually carved in stone. The Stèle of Revealing is doubly unusual in that the reverse side, usually undecorated, is also painted, with excerpts from *The Book of the Dead*, chapters 2 and 30 (the text of the obverse is from chapter 91). Concerning painted wooden stelæ in general, he remarks that «it is noteworthy that they all seem to originate from Thebes and its neighbourhood, and that their owners are mostly persons attached to the cults of Month and Amon.» He also notes that «a very interesting point about these stelæ is the evidence they afford for the religious views of the period. Most noteworthy is the identification of the forms of Rā-Horakhty [Ra-Hoor-Khuit] with Soker-Osiris.»[15]

The curator of the Boulaq Museum, M. Brugsch Bey, arranged for a French translation of the Egyptian text of the Stèle in the weeks preceding the writing of *Liber Legis* in 1904 E.V. Crowley translated the French into English, in verse form, and had this English versification of the hieroglyphic text at hand during the dictation of *Liber Legis*. In two instances (*Liber Legis* I:14, III:37-38) he had occasion to use it, but these verses do not appear in the MS. itself, having been inserted into the typescript prepared after the book's reception. Since the original Egyptian–French translation of the Stèle that Crowley paraphrased survives, and has a direct bearing upon the text of *Liber Legis*, it is given its first publication in Appendix A, with a new English translation by a qualified Egyptologist (Ph.D., Columbia), who chooses to remain anonymous. An actual photograph of the Stèle is also included; all previous appearances of the Stèle in Thelemic publications have been modern painted reproductions, based upon a copy made for Crowley by the Boulaq Museum.

[14] Abd el Hamid Zayed, «Painted Wooden Stelæ in the Cairo Museum,» *Revue d'égyptologie* 20 (1968), pp. 149–152, and plate 7.
[15] *Ibid.*

As remarked above, the manuscript of *Liber Legis* was written from direct-voice dictation on April 8–10, 1904 E.V., several weeks after the translation of the Stèle. The exact provenance of *Liber CCXX*, the edited form of *Liber XXXI*, is given in the following excerpt:

> Three typed copies [of *Liber Legis*] made in Cairo. One used by publishers of Zæhnsdorf edition (Chiswick Press) [*Thelema*][16] previous to rediscovery of MSS. Errors in vellum books [*Thelema*] due to the fact that this typescript not properly checked from MSS.»[17]

Thus, *Liber CCXX* had been edited and typed before Crowley left Egypt, but was later discovered to be unsatisfactory, since it had not been carefully compared to the manuscript. Such painstaking proofreading is of great importance with *Liber Legis*—the book insists upon exact redaction—but was impossible after Crowley's return to England since he misplaced the manuscript. The flaws in this early form of *Liber CCXX* were only discovered after its first publication in 1909 E.V., upon recovery of the manuscript. *Liber XXXI* and *Liber CCXX* were later published in *The Equinox*, marking *Liber XXXI*'s first publication, and the first appearance of *Liber CCXX* as Crowley intended it.[18]

The many injunctions in *Liber Legis* concerning its editing prompted the creation of a new class of magical literature—Class «A», which «consists of books of which may be changed not so much as the style of a letter.»[19] A salient feature of *Liber Legis*, when considered in context with the other books in this volume, is that it was *not* the work of Aleister Crowley, as Crowley himself emphasizes:

---

[16] Θελημα (London: privately printed, 1909), 3 vols. Produced for Crowley by the Chiswick Press and Zæhnsdorf, it was printed with gold borders on vellum and bound in parchment. Crowley's copy had the three volumes bound in one.

[17] Norman Mudd, *Notes of Conversations with Aleister Crowley concerning the Book of the Law*, unpublished typescript, O.T.O. Archives.

[18] For *Liber XXXI* see *The Equinox* I(7), 1912, facing p. 386 *ff*. For *Liber CCXX* see *The Equinox* I(10), 1913, pp. 9–33.

[19] Crowley, «A Syllabus of the Official Instructions of A.˙.A.˙. Hitherto Published,» *The Equinox* I(10), 1913, p. 43. For definitions of the classes see Appendix B *infra*.

I claim authorship even of all the other A.˙.A.˙. Books in Class
A, though I wrote them inspired beyond all I know to be I. Yet
in these Books did Aleister Crowley, the master of English both
in prose and in verse, partake insofar as he was That. Compare
those Books with *The Book of the Law*! The style [of the
former] is simple and sublime; the imagery is gorgeous and
faultless; the rhythm is subtle and intoxicating; the theme is
interpreted in faultless symphony.   There are no errors of
grammar, no infelicities of phrase. Each Book is perfect in its
kind.

I, daring to snatch credit for these [. . .] dared nowise to lay
claim to have touched *The Book of the Law*, not with my littlest
finger-tip.[20]

In his Commentaries on *Liber Legis* Crowley enlarges on this
important point:

[T]he use of such un-English expressions makes a clear-cut
distinction between AIWAZ and the Scribe.  In the inspired
Books, such as *Liber LXV, VII, DCCCXIII* and others, written
by The Beast 666 directly, not from dictation, no such awkward
expressions are to be found.  The style shows a well-marked
difference.[21]

The « inspired Books » referred to above constitute, with *Liber
Legis*, the Holy Books of Thelema. *Liber Legis* took Crowley very
much by surprise.  He was only twenty-eight when he received it,
and although possessed of experience in esotericism through his
membership in the Hermetic Order of the Golden Dawn, he was at
its reception disinclined to magical studies.  A full grasp of *Liber
Legis'* significance came only after further initiations.  In fact, three
decades passed before Crowley issued the account of the reception of
*Liber Legis* stipulated by the book in 1904 E.V.[22]

The Holy Books received three years later in 1907 E.V. were fruit
of his early magical career as a connected whole, entailing years of
initiations and applied study in several magical and mystical
disciplines.  Crowley himself illustrates this in a hitherto-unpublished

---

[20] Crowley, *The Equinox of the Gods*, p. 106.

[21] Crowley, commentary to *Liber Legis* III:46.

[22] See *Liber Legis* III:39, page 125 *infra*.   The account referred to is *The Equinox of the Gods*, issued by O.T.O. in 1936 E.V.

chronology reproduced in full on the following page. For its first publication, references have been provided to Crowley's accounts of the episodes cited, as published in his *Confessions*.[23] Obscure or abbreviated entries have been expanded within editorial brackets.

Terse as this document is, it is remarkably comprehensive. Beginning with his first tentative enquiries into occultism at age 22, it follows the high points of his early career through the fall of 1907 E.V. The chronology lists Crowley's initiations in the Hermetic Order of the Golden Dawn from grades $0° = 0°$ through $5° = 6°$, and after a passing reference to the leadership crisis that sundered the Order in 1900 E.V., it documents his private studies and initiations (grades $6° = 5°$ and $7° = 4°$). It ends with the words «Books begin to be received at will», a reference to the series of Holy Books whose reception commenced in October of 1907 E.V. In this year Crowley took the oath of the grade of Magister Templi $8° = 3°$, which he attained fully several years later. His motto was Vi Veri Vniversum Vivus Vici («By the force of Truth I have conquered the Universe while living»). Abbreviated as V.V.V.V.V., it occurs throughout these Holy Books: it was the magical motto the prophet used «in His office of giving out the ‹Official Books of A.˙.A.˙.› to the world in *The Equinox*.»[24] With the writing of these Holy Books through his physical vehicle, Aleister Crowley, V.V.V.V.V. manifested a link with the «Secret Chiefs» of Ordo A.˙.A.˙., and conveyed the authority necessary for Crowley to fill the leadership vacuum in its dependent Orders, the R.R. et A.C. and the Golden Dawn. This is recounted in *Liber LXI Vel Causæ*, in a passage with special relevance to these Holy Books:

> 29. Also one V.V.V.V.V. arose, an exalted adept of the rank of Master of the Temple (or this much He disclosed to the Exempt Adepts) and His utterance is enshrined in the Sacred Writings.
>
> 30. Such are Liber Legis, Liber Cordis Cincti Serpente, Liber Liberi vel Lapidis Lazuli and such others whose existence may one day be divulged unto you. Beware lest you

---

[23] Crowley, *The Confessions of Aleister Crowley* (London: Cape, and New York: Hill & Wang, 1969; also reprinted in London and Boston: Routledge & Kegan Paul, 1979).

[24] Crowley, *The Equinox of the Gods*, p. 86n.

## I   *The Augur*

| 1898 [E.V.] | March | [Read *The*] Book of Bl[ac]k Magic [and of Pacts]* (had been skimming Alchemy) | 126–7 |
|---|---|---|---|
| | April | [Read *The*] Cloud [*up*]on [*the*] Sanctuary† | 127, 145–8 |
| | July | [Read *The*] Q[abalah (*sic*), read: Kabbalah] Unveiled ‡ | 164 |
| | Aug. | Met [Julian] Baker | 164–5 |
| | Oct. | Met [George Cecil] Jones — [Read *The Sacred Magic of*] Abramelin [*the Mage*]§ | 172–3 |

## II   *The Sun*

| 1898 | Nov. 18 | $0° = 0^{\square}$ | ⊛ [Spirit] vision starts | 176, 224–5 |
|---|---|---|---|---|
| | Dec. | $1° = 10^{\square}$ | Beginning Ceremonial Magic | 178–82 |
| 1899 | Jan. | $2° = 9^{\square}$ | Met Allan Bennett | 177–81 |
| | Feb. | $3° = 8^{\square}$ | | 178 |
| | May | $4° = 7^{\square}$ | Met [S.L. MacGregor] Mathers | 178 |

## III   *The Sorcerer*

| 1899 | Oct. | To Boleskine preparing Abr[amelin Operation] | 184, 190–3 |
|---|---|---|---|
| 1900 | Jan. | $5° = 6^{\square}$ | 193–5 |
| | March | Row in G∴D∴ | 193–7 |

## IV   *The Magician*

| 1900 | June | To Mexico. All ceremonial. ($6° = 5^{\square}$) | 202–4 |
|---|---|---|---|

## V   *The Adept*

| 1901 | Jan. | Beginning Concentration | 213–4 |
|---|---|---|---|
| | Aug. | With Allan [Bennett] — Raja Yoga & Philosophy | 234–49 |
| 1902 | Sept. | Results in R[aja] Y[oga] | 247–9 |
| 1904 | April | Egypt Revelation — [Received] *Liber Legis* | 393–4, 469–70 |
| 1906 | Jan. | $7° = 4^{\square}$   Using all methods. | 445, 509–17 |

## VI   *The Magi*

| 1906 | Oct. | Nirvikalpa Samadhi | 532–33 |
|---|---|---|---|
| 1907 | Oct. | **Books begin to be received at will** [*emphasis added*] | 559 |

---

\* A.E. Waite, *The Book of Black Magic and of Pacts* (London: G. Redway, 1898). [Reissued with revisions as *The Book of Ceremonial Magic*.]

† Karl von Eckarthausen, *The Cloud upon the Sanctuary*, trans. I. De Steiger (London: G. Redway, 1896).

‡ Knorr von Rosenroth, *Kabbala Denudata; the Kabbalah Unveiled* [*Zohar*], trans. S.L. MacGregor Mathers (London: G. Redway, 1887).

§ Abraham ben Simeon, *The Sacred Magic of Abramelin the Mage*, trans. S.L. MacGregor Mathers (London: J.M. Watkins, 1898).

interpret them either in the Light or in the darkness, for
only in L.V.X. may they be understood.

31. Also He conferred upon D.D.S., O.M., and another, the
Authority of the Triad, who in turn have delegated it unto
others, and they yet again, so that the Body of Initiates may
be perfect, even from the Crown unto the Kingdom and
beyond.[25]

Crowley writes that the « function of the Magister Templi is to
cause the desert to blossom by transmitting the Logos of the Æon to
those that are below the Abyss.»[26] Thus in 1907 E.V. many Holy
Books were transmitted through the hand of Aleister Crowley, as is
detailed below by Major General J.F.C. Fuller, who refers to
Crowley by his Neophyte motto, Frater Perdurabo:

Of V.V.V.V.V. we have no information. We do not know,
and it is of no importance that we should know, whether he is
an actual person or a magical projection of Frater P[erdurabo],
or identical with Aiwass, or anything else [ . . . ] It is sufficient
to say that all the Class A publications of the A.˙.A.˙. should be
regarded as not only verbally and liberally [sic] inspired by
Him, but that this accuracy should be taken to extend even to
the style of the letter. If a word is unexpectedly spelt with a
capital letter, it must not be thought that this is a mistake; there
is some serious reason why it should be so. During this year
1907, therefore, we find a number of such books dictated by
him to Frater P. Of the sublimity of these books no words can
give expression. It will be noticed that they are totally different
in style from Liber Legis, just as both of them are different from
any of the writings of Frater P.[27]

In his Confessions Crowley gives an account of the writing of these
books from the point of view of the scribe:

[T]he spirit came upon me and I wrote a number of books in a
way which I hardly know how to describe. They were not

[25] See Liber LXI Vel Causæ immediately following the Synopsis, infra.
[26] Crowley, Preliminary Analysis of Liber LXV, IV:61. For bibliographic references
to the several editions of the commentaries see Appendix C infra.
[27] J.F.C. Fuller, « The Temple of Solomon the King,» The Equinox I(9), 1913, pp.
7–8.

taken from dictation like *The Book of the Law* nor were they my
own composition. I cannot even call them automatic writing. I
can only say that I was not wholly conscious at the time of what
I was writing, and I felt that I had no right to «change» so
much as the style of a letter. They were written with the utmost
rapidity without pausing for thought for a single moment, and I
have not presumed to revise them. Perhaps «plenary inspiration» is the only adequate phrase, and this has become so
discredited that people are loth to admit the possibility of such a
thing.

The prose of these books, the chief of which are *Liber Cordis
Cincti Serpente* [*Liber LXV*] [...] and *Liberi Vel Lapidis
Lazuli* [*Liber VII*], is wholly different from anything that I
have written myself. It is characterized by a sustained sublimity
of which I am totally incapable and it overrides all the
intellectual objections which I should myself have raised. It
does not admit the need to explain itself to anyone, even to me. I
cannot doubt that these books are the work of an intelligence
independent of my own.[28]

There are many subtleties among these Holy Books, both of degree
of inspiration and mode of reception. Crowley especially cherished
*Libri VII* and *LXV*, but all of these Holy Books were penned during
high trance. General Fuller's account elucidates this aspect of their
reception:

We may turn for a moment to consider the actual conditions
under which he received them. We find the hint of the nature
of the communication in *Liber LXV* and *Liber VII*. On one or
two occasions the scribe introduced his thought upon the note, in
particular *Liber VII*, Chapter I, Verse 30, where Verse 29
suggested Verse 30 to Frater P., who wrote it consciously and
was corrected in Verse 31. Frater P. is, however, less
communicative about this writing than about *Liber Legis*. It
appears that during the whole period of writing he was actually
in Samadhi, although, strangely enough, he did not know it
himself. It is a question of the transference of the Ego from the
personal to the impersonal. He, the conscious human man,
could not say «I am in Samadhi»; he was merely conscious that
«that which was he» was in Samadhi.[29]

---

[28] *The Confessions of Aleister Crowley*, p. 559.
[29] J.F.C. Fuller, *op. cit.*, p. 8.

An entry for 1:30 a.m. of October 30 in Crowley's *Diary for 1907 E.V.* records *Liber VII*'s reception: «About 11 [p.m. of October 29] (I suppose) I began. the 7 fold Word & finished the same.»[30] This confirms Crowley's assertion that these books were «written with the utmost rapidity without pausing for thought for a single moment.» *Liber VII*, a book of over 5700 words, was written in only 2½ hours. For comparative purposes, *Liber VII* is slightly longer than the MS. of *Liber Legis*, which was taken from dictation in 3 hours.

The *Diary* also records the writing of *Liber LXV* immediately after *Liber VII*'s reception. Unlike *Liber VII*, this book was written a chapter or two at a time over several days, from the evening of October 30 through the 3rd of November. The following excerpt sheds further light on the process by which these books were written:

> Wrote [Chapters] I & II *Liber Cordis Cincti Serpente* [*Liber LXV*] again no shadow of Samadhi; only a feeling that V.V.V.V.V. was in His Samadhi, and writing by my pen. *i.e.* the pen of the scribe, and that scribe not οὐ μή, who reasons etc. nor a[leister] c[rowley] who is a poet & selects; but of some perfectly passive person.[31]

After the writing of *Libri VII* and *LXV*, V.V.V.V.V. issued several more Holy Books, whose reception is recorded in the *Diary*. The first of these, *Liber LXVI*, was received several weeks later on November 25.

Crowley's rather obscure *Diary* entries recording the reception of portions of *Liber CCXXXI* show that the «Arcana in Atus of Tahuti» and the «Sigils of genii &c.» were received on December 5–6; the «Sigilla 22» were copied on December 14. It appears that the textual portion of *Liber CCXXXI* was received several years later, as is discussed below.

During December 12–14 Crowley received a new book each day—*Libri X, CD,* and *XXVII.* He writes in his 1908 E.V. diary that *Liber DCCCXIII* was «delivered unto me in the winter of last year»; it was therefore received in the winter of 1907–08 E.V.[32]

---

[30] Crowley, Diary for 1907 E.V., holograph MS. Published with editorial abridgements in *Sex and Religion* (Nashville: Thelema Publishing Co., 1981), p. 160.

[31] *Ibid.*

[32] Crowley, *John St. John*, special supplement to *The Equinox* I(1), 1909, p. 133.

The balance of the Holy Books were apparently received in 1911 E.V. In his *Confessions*, Crowley lists several Holy Books in a survey of writings produced in that year.[33] This list includes *Liber CCXXXI*, discussed above—an apparent reference to the versified textual portion of that book, which is not mentioned in the *Diary for 1907 E.V.* Also listed are *Libri I, XC, CLVI* and *CCCLXX*. However, Crowley mistakenly lists *Libri X, LXVI* and *CD*, all of which were actually written in 1907 E.V. Such confusion is understandable since Crowley had lost his diaries for both 1907 and 1911 E.V., and was writing from memory for *The Confessions* roughly a decade later.

Having reviewed the provenance of the Holy Books, a technical digression is necessary here to resolve a long-standing problem of attribution. In spite of their spiritual provenance, as detailed above, many students hold that Crowley considered only *five* of these inspired writings to be Holy Books. How this belief obtained will require some explanation.

Although a full and proper account of A∴A∴ is impossible in this place—readers are referred to the widely-available authorized account, «One Star in Sight»[34]—it will be useful here to discuss those customs of A∴A∴ that bear upon the identity of the Holy Books.

The official publications of A∴A∴ are grouped into five classes, from «A» to «E». The classification system was devised to obviate potential confusion regarding the relative sanctity or authority of the books and papers evaluated, and has generally succeeded in this. Class «A», by definition, «consists of books of which may be changed not so much as the style of a letter: that is, they represent the utterance of an Adept entirely beyond the criticism of even the Visible Head of the Organization.» This class ultimately derives from the first and foremost of the Holy Books, *Liber Legis*, and Crowley extended it to the twelve inspired books received from V.V.V.V.V.[35] It is extremely

---

[33] *The Confessions of Aleister Crowley*, pp. 673–74.

[34] Crowley, *Magick in Theory in Practice* (New York: Dover, 1976) pp. 229–44. For earlier editions see Appendix C.

[35] Crowley, «Syllabus,» pp. 43–46.

unlikely that Crowley would intentionally qualify the «holiness» of books in Class «A»—their very definition argues against it.

The source of the problem of attribution is Crowley's rarest and most prized private edition, *Thelema*.[36] Published in 1909 E.V., *Thelema* included *Liber LXI* and five of the Holy Books—*Libri VII, XXVII, LXV, CCXX* and *DCCCXIII*. Many bibliographers list it as *The Holy Books*, although the only title the edition bears is *Thelema*. Crowley himself used the proper title—his diaries abound in references to *Thelema*, which he often used for bibliomancy. One of Crowley's references to the Holy Books could be construed to mean the three volumes of *Thelema*, but does not imply exclusive equivalence when taken in context.[37] As a rule, he used the term «Holy Books» generically.

Crowley issued the three volumes of *Thelema* one by one, as students in A.˙.A.˙. achieved successive grades in the Outer College of the Order.[38] By his account, on entering the Order the Probationer received the first volume, comprised of «*Liber LXI* and the secret holy book, *Liber LXV*.»[39] (Note that Crowley does not term *Liber LXI* a Holy Book.) Those who passed to Neophyte received the second volume, which included *Liber VII*. In a like manner, *Liber CCXX* was given to the Zelator, *Liber XXVII* to the Practicus and *Liber DCCCXIII* to the Philosophus.[40] Thus, the books in *Thelema* comprise the core curriculum of aspirants in the Outer College of A.˙.A.˙..

The notion that the term «Holy Book» should be reserved for the books published in *Thelema* rests on the assumption that a Class «A» book must form a part of the graded curriculum of A.˙.A.˙. in order to be so termed. It is a simple matter to dismiss this notion on its own terms. Although the basic assumption may well be correct, *Thelema*'s equivalence with the Holy Books is clearly erroneous.

---

[36] See note 16 above.
[37] See *Astarté Vel Liber Berylli Sub Figurâ CLXXV*, §19, *The Equinox* I(7), 1912, pp. 37–58.
[38] *Liber Collegii Sancti Sub Figurâ CLXXXV* (London: privately published, 1909).
[39] Crowley, *Book Four* (Dallas: Sangreal Publications, 1972), p. 127.
[40] Crowley, *Preliminary Analysis of Liber LXV* I:1. The relevant passage is excerpted in the Synopsis, *infra*, under the heading «Liber LXV».

A colophon note to *Liber CCCLXX* attributes it to the grade of Dominus Liminus, thus resuming the A.'.A.'. graded curriculum where *Thelema* left off at the preceding grade of Practicus.[41] The Holy Books published in *Thelema* had similar notes appended to them; for comparative purposes, these notes have been transferred to the Synopsis in the present edition. *Liber I*, attributed by Crowley to Adeptus Minor, was termed a Holy Book by Crowley himself.[42] Both examples were written after *Thelema*'s publication.

In later years Crowley relaxed the secrecy with which he shrouded these books. *Liber Legis* was republished, and *The Equinox* III(1) included *Libri LXI* and *LXV*.[43] Crowley planned to issue the remainder of *Thelema* in subsequent numbers of Volume III, but the publishing program failed—*The Equinox* III(2), which included *Liber VII*, only survives in galley proofs.[44]

Thus, the confusion Crowley took such pains to forestall arose after his death due to the confusion of a bibliographic reference (the book *Thelema*) with an ill-defined tradition concerning the Holy Books. An illustration of the effect of this loose definition is a recent edition comprised of three books excerpted from *Thelema*. Entitled *The Holy Books*, it led many students to believe that only three Class «A» writings are Holy Books.[45] Its editor, Dr. F.I. Regardie, acknowledges the error, and suggests *Three Holy Books* as a more accurate title. Given such candor, it is only fair to add that *Five Holy Books* would be a better popular subtitle for *Thelema* itself.

Two of the books in the present volume have had classification changes. *Liber I* was first published as Class «B», the class reserved for works of «ordinary scholarship, enlightened and earnest.» It was later listed as Class «A» in the official syllabus published in 1913 E.V. [46] This, taken with Crowley's explicit reference to it as a Holy

---

[41] Crowley, «Curriculum of A.'.A.'.,» *The Equinox* III(1), 1919, pp. 18–38. See also *Liber CCCLXX* in *The Equinox* I(6), 1911, pp. 33–39; the note is excerpted in the Synopsis, *infra*, under the heading «Liber CCCLXX».

[42] Crowley, *Preliminary Analysis of Liber LXV*, V:51.

[43] *The Equinox* III(1), 1919, pp. 53–98.

[44] Crowley, «Præmonstrance of A.'.A.'.,» *The Equinox* III(1), 1919, pp. 12–13.

[45] *The Holy Books* (Dallas: Sangreal Publications, 1972).

[46] See imprimatur to *Liber I* in *The Equinox* I(7), 1912, p. 6. Compare the listing in Crowley, «Syllabus,» p. 43.

Book, prompts its inclusion as Class « A » in the present compilation. Another book, *Liber LXI*, was first published in *Thelema*, where it appeared in Class « A ». It was changed to Class « B » in the 1913 E.V. syllabus, and changed yet again in 1919 E.V., when it was republished in Class « D », signifying an official ritual or instruction.[47] Crowley considered *Liber LXI* an « introduction to the series »;[48] it is therefore included as the Introduction to the present edition, under its most recent imprimatur in Class « D ».

Also, three books *containing* Class « A » material have been excluded from the present compilation.

The first two may be treated together. They are *Liber CDXV— Opus Lutetianum* (commonly called *The Paris Working*) and *Liber CDXVIII—Liber XXX ÆRUM Vel Sæculi* (commonly called *The Vision and the Voice*).[49] Both are diary records of magical workings conducted by Crowley in collaboration with Victor B. Neuburg. Crowley placed these two books in Class « AB », which he reserved for Class « A » material contained in a Class « B » text. Although Crowley regarded both books with reverence, it appears that he did not consider these « composite » class writings to be Holy Books. The Class « A » material, typically the utterance of a deific or angelic entity, is inextricably imbedded in the Class « B » text, often without benefit of quotation marks. Evidence for this view may be found in Crowley's writings, where he clearly distinguishes *Liber CDXVIII* from the Holy Books as a group.[50] Also, *Liber CDXVIII* has two sections pertaining to Class « D », since they comprise official rituals or instructions.[51]

The third book excluded is in Class « A–B »: *Liber Θεσαυρου*

---

[47] See the listing in Crowley, « Syllabus », p. 47. Compare to *Liber LXI*'s imprimatur in *The Equinox* III(1), 1919, p. 54.

[48] Crowley, « Syllabus », p. 54.

[49] *Liber CDXV* was published as « The Paris Working » in *Sex and Religion* (Nashville: Thelema Publishing Co, 1981), pp. 169–223. *Liber CDXVIII* was first published as a special supplement to *The Equinox* I(5), 1910, and was first issued with Crowley's commentary as *Liber XXX Ærum Vel Sæculi Sub Figurâ CDXVIII* [ . . . ] *The Vision and the Voice* (Barstow, Calif.: Thelema Publishing Co., 1952). For other editions see Appendix C.

[50] Crowley, *Preliminary Analysis of Liber LXV*, IV:59-62; see also *Book Four*, p. 88.

[51] See Appendix B under *Libri CDXVIII* and *VIII*.

'Εἴδολον *Sub Figurâ CMLXIII*, commonly called *The Treasure-House of Images*.[52] In this case, only a short prefatory note is in Class « A »; the book itself, in Class « B », is the work of Major General J.F.C. Fuller.

And what of the future? Will additional writings of this kind be received by others? Suffice to say that the Knowledge and Conversation of the Holy Guardian Angel is the central (though not final) goal of aspirants to A∴A∴.. Crowley's communion with his Angel, Aiwass, reached tangible expression in these Holy Books, and he strove mightily to help others attain to this spiritual experience. As the following excerpt shows, he did expect similar communications to be received by those who succeeded in this, the Great Work:

> Although it [*Liber Legis*] was not the direct result of invocation, unless the successful invocation of Horus be accounted such, yet in view of the Magical tradition that communications of this type may and should result more or less directly from the use of ceremonial methods, and of the absence of any other reasonable theory which covers the facts, I am led to make experiments and to induce others to make experiments on the assumption that people trained in a) Magical b) Mystical c) Qabalistic arts are more likely than those not so trained to receive similar communications with such fulness and accuracy as enables them to withstand the severest criticism. (The original communication was made to Rose [Crowley] but would obviously have come to nothing had I not been there to gestate and parturate the seed.) These experiments have been justified by such results as the books *LXV, VII, 418, I, Ararita*, and by such work as the editing of the *T[ao] T[eh] K[ing]* and the *Y[i] K[ing]*. The validity of the methods is demonstrated by *J[ohn] S[t.] J[ohn]*.[53] Also by the success of those who have put them into practice with fidelity, energy and intelligence. Indirectly also by the quality of the failures and disasters which have accompanied

[52] J.F.C. Fuller, Θεσαυρου 'Εἴδολον *Sub Figurâ CMLXIII*, *The Treasure-House of Images*, special supplement to *The Equinox* I(3), 1910.

[53] *Libri I, LXV, VII* and *Ararita* [*Liber DCCCXIII*] are included in the present volume. For *Liber 418* see Note 49 *supra*. See also the *Tao Teh King* (Kings Beach, Calif.: Thelema Publications, 1975) and *Shih Yi* [*Yi King*], (Oceanside, Calif.: Thelema Publications, 1971). For *John St. John* see *The Equinox* I(1), 1909, special supplement.

experiments conducted in ways which I disapprove. Incidental-
ly I have been able to predict results both of the wise and foolish
virgins under my supervision. [ ... ] [I]t is my special
business to set people to obtain the K[nowledge] and C[onversa-
tion] of the H[oly] G[uardian] A[ngel] by such means as I
have myself proved valid. By the word « conversation » I
understand communication similar to *The Book of the Law* as to
origin, authority and value, each as may be suited to the nature
and T[rue] Will of the aspirant or experimenter.[54]

Crowley's last remark deserves special emphasis. Several purported « Holy Books » have appeared over the years that superficially
resemble those received by Crowley in style and format, a feature that
does not necessarily connote authenticity. Few, if indeed any, show
much more than the literary fecundity of their authors. Inspired
writings are a spontaneous by-product of the spiritual attainments they
reflect, not ends in themselves. Also, they have no equivalence with
the results of simple mediumship—years of aspiration and rigorous
training were a prerequisite even for a mystic and magician of
Crowley's abundant native gifts. But such directly-inspired writings
have been received in the past—Blake's reception of *Jerusalem* is the
classic Western precursor—and Crowley clearly expected more to be
produced in the future.

For the present compilation, in certain respects an updated second
edition of the collection published in 1909 E.V., the original title of
*Thelema* is retained, and popular usage is acknowledged in the subtitle
*The Holy Books of Thelema.* All writings in Class « A » (except for
« composite » material, as discussed above) are considered Holy
Books. Should this prove to be an error despite the available
evidence, it will be corrected in a future edition. The Holy Books
have been collected and republished verbatim from the sources cited
in Appendix C. Extraneous commentaries in the original publications
have generally been transferred to the Synopsis. Material in editorial
brackets appearing *within* a text (as occurs in *Libri XXVII, CCXXXI*
and *CD*) is retained; the reader is advised that these are not insertions
by the present editor. Also, the use of typographical conventions such
as ligatures (Æ, œ, fi, *etc.*) has been made consistent.

---

[54] Norman Mudd, *op. cit.*

An explanation of the A.˙.A.˙. classification system appears in the Technical Bibliography (Appendix B), which also lists the technical books and papers of Thelema by number, class and title. This is intended to help readers place the Class « A » material in context with writings in other classes.

Crowley wrote several commentaries to individual Holy Books, many of which have been published. The reader may consult the Selected References in Appendix C for bibliographic information.

It is to be hoped that the publication of these books, here collected in one volume for the first time, will assist all aspirants in the accomplishment of their True Wills, the Great Work, the Summum Bonum, True Wisdom and Perfect Happiness.

*Love is the law, love under will.*

### ῾ΥΜΕΝΑΙΟΣ Α

*Hymenæus Alpha 777, Caliph*
X° O.T.O.

Maj. Grady Louis McMurtry
*(U.S. Army Reserve)*

Berkeley, California
☉ in ♌, ☽ in ♉
An IIIxii
August 12, 1982 E.V.

# SYNOPSIS

[This Synopsis has been compiled from Aleister Crowley's writings; sources are referenced at the end of the Synopsis. Crowley's explanation of the meaning of the title and/or number ascribed to each book follows each description. Publishing histories and full bibliographic information for the books described may be found in Appendices B and C. ED.]

## INTRODUCTION

### LIBER LXI

*Liber Causæ.* The Preliminary Lection, including the History Lection.

Explains the actual history of the origin of the present movement. Its statements are accurate in the ordinary sense of the word. The object of the book is to discount mythopœia.[1]

A manuscript giving an account of the history of the A.'.A.'. in recent times.

This history contains no mythology; it is a statement of facts susceptible of rational proof.[2]

> *LXI*    See *Sepher Sephiroth.** The allusion is to the fact that this book forms an introduction to the series.[3]

## THE HOLY BOOKS

### LIBER I

*Liber B Vel Magi*

This is an account of the Grade of Magus, the highest grade which it is ever possible to manifest in any way whatever upon this plane. Or so it is said by the Masters of the Temple.[1]

---

* *The Equinox* I(8), 1912, special supplement.

*The Book of the Magus*

This is an inspired writing. It describes the conditions of that exalted Grade. I had at this time no idea that I should ever attain to it; in fact, I thought it utterly beyond possibility. This book was given to me that I might avoid mistakes when the time came for me to become a Magus. It is impossible to give any idea of the terror and sublimity of this book, while the accuracy of its predictions and of its descriptions of the state of being, at that time wholly beyond my imagination to conceive, make it a most astonishing document.[4]

*I*    I is the number of the Magus in the Tarot.[3]

## LIBER VII

*Liber Liberi Vel Lapidis Lazuli, Adumbratio Kabbalæ Ægyptiorum Sub Figurâ VII*, being the Voluntary Emancipation of a certain Exempt Adept from his Adeptship. These are the Birth Words of a Master of the Temple.

The nature of this book is sufficiently explained by its title. Its seven chapters are referred to the seven planets in the following order: Mars, Saturn, Jupiter, Sol, Mercury, Luna, Venus.[1]

*The Book of Lapis Lazuli*

Gives in magical language an account of the Initiation of a Master of the Temple. This is the only parallel, for Beauty of Ecstasy, to *Liber LXV*.[2]

The full knowledge of the interpretation of this book is concealed from all save only the Sixfold Star.

The Neophyte must nevertheless acquire a copy and thoroughly acquaint himself with the contents. He must commit one chapter to memory.[5]

*VII*    Refers to the 7 chapters, and to the fact that the number 7 is peculiarly suitable to the subject of the Book.[3]

## LIBER X

*Liber Porta Lucis*

This book is an account of the sending forth of the Master by the A∴A∴ and an explanation of his mission.[1]

This book is called *The Gate of Light*. It explains how those who have attained initiation, taking pity upon the darkness and minuteness of the earth, send forth a messenger to men. The message follows. It is an appeal to those who, being developed beyond the average of their fellows, see fit to take up the Great Work. This Work is then described in general terms with a few hints of its conditions.[4]

X       Porta Lucis, the Gate of Light, is one of the titles of
        Malkuth, whose number is X.[3]

## LIBER XXVII

*Liber Trigrammaton*, being a book of Trigrams of the Mutations of the TAO with the YIN and the YANG.

An account of the cosmic process: corresponding to the Stanzas of DZYAN in another system.[1]

*Vel Trigrammaton*

It describes the Course of Creation under the Figure of the Interplay of Three Principles. The book corresponding to the Stanzas of Dzyan.[2]

The full knowledge of the interpretation of this book is concealed from all.

The Practicus must nevertheless acquire a copy, thoroughly acquaint himself with the contents, and commit them to memory.[5]

*XXVII*     The number of permutations of 3 things taken 3 at a
            time, and (of course) the cube of 3.[3]

## LIBER LXV

*Liber Cordis Cincti Serpente*

An account of the relations of the Aspirant with his Holy Guardian Angel. This book is given to Probationers, as the attainment of the Knowledge and Conversation of the Holy Guardian Angel is the Crown of the Outer College. Similarly *Liber VII* is given to Neophytes, as the grade of Master of the Temple is the next resting-place, and *Liber CCXX* to Zelator, since that carries him to the highest of all possible grades. *Liber XXVII* is given to the Practicus, as in this book is the ultimate foundation of the highest theoretical Qabalah, and *Liber DCCCXIII* to the Philosophus, as it is the foundation of the highest practical Qabalah.[1]

*The Book of the Heart Girt with a Serpent*

This magical treatise describes particularly the relation of the Aspirant with his Higher Self. It is, alike in conception and execution, a masterpiece of exaltation of thought, carved in Pure Beauty.[2]

The five chapters refer to the five Elements. 1–Earth, 2–Air, 3–Water, 4–Fire, and 5–Spirit. Each shows its Element in the light of the relation between the Adeptus Minor and his Holy Guardian Angel.[6]

The full knowledge of the interpretation of this book is concealed from all, save only the Shining Triangle.

The Probationer must nevertheless acquire a copy and thoroughly acquaint himself with the contents. He must commit one chapter to memory.[5]

LXV     The number of Adonai.[3]

## LIBER LXVI

*Liber Stellæ Rubeæ.* A secret ritual, the Heart of IAO-OAI, delivered unto V.V.V.V.V. for his use in a certain matter of *Liber Legis*, and written down under the figure LXVI.

This book is sufficiently described by the title.[1]

*The Book of the Ruby Star*

[D]escribes an extremely powerful ritual of practical Magick; how to arouse the Magical Force within the operator and how to use it to create whatever may be required.[4]

LXVI     The sum of the first 11 numbers. This book relates to Magic, whose Key is 11.[3]

## LIBER XC

*Liber TZADDI Vel Hamus Hermeticus Sub Figurâ XC*

An account of Initiation, and an indication as to those who are suitable for the same.[1]

*The Book of the Hermetic Fish-Hook*
[S]ummons mankind to undertake the Great Work. It describes the conditions of initiation and its results in language of great poetic power.[4]

XC          Tzaddi means a fish-hook. «I will make you fishers of men.»[3]

## LIBER CLVI

*Liber Cheth Vel Vallum Abiegni Sub Figurâ CLVI*
This book is a perfect account of the task of the Exempt Adept, considered under the symbols of a particular plane, not the intellectual.[1]

*The Wall of Abiegnus*
*The Wall of Abiegnus* (the Sacred Mountain of the Rosicrucians) gives the formula of Attainment by devotion to our Lady Babalon. It instructs the aspirant how to dissolve his personality in the Universal Life.[4]

CLVI          Babalon, to whom the book refers. See *Sepher Sephiroth*.[3]

## LIBER CCXX

*Liber AL Vel Legis Sub Figurâ CCXX* as delivered by LXXVIII unto DCLXVI
This book is the foundation of the new Æon, and thus of the whole of our Work.[1]

In this revelation is the basis of the future Æon. Within the memory of man we have had the Pagan period, the worship of Nature, of Isis, of the Mother, of the Past; the Christian period, the worship of Man, of Osiris, of the Present. The first period is simple, quiet, easy, and pleasant; the material ignores the spiritual; the second is of suffering and death: the spiritual strives to ignore the material. Christianity and all cognate religions worship death, glorify suffering, deify corpses. The new Æon is the worship of the spiritual made one with the material, of Horus, of the Child, of the Future.

Isis was Liberty; Osiris, bondage; but the new Liberty is that of Horus. Osiris conquered her because she did not understand him.

Horus avenges both his Father and his Mother. This child Horus is a twin, two in one. Horus and Harpocrates are one, and they are also one with Set or Apophis, the destroyer of Osiris. It is by the destruction of the principle of death that they are born. The establishment of this new Æon, this new fundamental principle, is the great work now to be accomplished in the world.[7]

To recapitulate the historical basis of *The Book of the Law*, let me say that evolution (within human memory) shows three great steps:

1. the worship of the Mother, when the universe was conceived as simple nourishment drawn directly from her;
2. the worship of the Father, when the universe was imagined as catastrophic;
3. the worship of the Child, in which we come to perceive events as a continual growth partaking in its elements of both these methods.[8]

Generally, *The Book of the Law* claims to answer all possible religious problems. One is struck by the fact that so many of them are stated and settled separately in so short a space.[9]

It reconciles cosmological conceptions which transcend time and space with a conventional, historical point of view. In the first place it announces unconditional truth, but in the second is careful to state that the «Magical Formula» (or system of principles) on which the practical part of the book is based is not an absolute truth but one relative to the terrestrial time of the revelation. (It is a strong point in favour of the Book that it makes no pretence to settle the practical problems of humanity once and for all. It contents itself with indicating a stage in evolution.)[10]

The full knowledge of the interpretation of this book is concealed from all.

The Zelator must nevertheless acquire a copy and thoroughly acquaint himself with the contents. He must commit one chapter to memory.[5]

CCXX  The number of the Verses in the three chapters of the Book. It has, however, an enormous amount of symbolism; in particular it combines the 10 Sephiroths and 22 Paths; 78 is איוס. For 666 vide *Sepher Sephiroth*.[3]

## Liber XXXI

*AL (Liber Legis), The Book of the Law Sub Figurâ XXXI* as delivered by 93—Aiwass—418 to Ankh-f-n-khonsu, The Priest of the Princes who is 666[11]

I, a master of English, was made to take down in three hours, from dictation, sixty-five 8″ × 10″ pages of words not only strange, but often displeasing to me in themselves; concealing in cipher propositions unknown to me, majestic and profound; foretelling events public and private beyond my control, or that of any man.

This Book proves: there is a Person thinking and acting in a præterhuman manner, either without a body of flesh, or with the power of communicating telepathically with men and inscrutably directing their actions.[12]

## Liber CCXXXI

*Liber Arcanorum τ*ων *ATU* του *Tahuti Quas Vidit Asar in Amennti Sub Figurâ CCXXXI Liber Carcerorum* των *Qliphoth cum suis Geniis. Adduntur Sigilla et Nomina Eorum.*

This is an account of the cosmic process so far as it is indicated by the Tarot Trumps.[1]

*Liber CCXXXI (XXII Domarum et XXII Carcerorum)*[13]

*Liber CCXXXI* is a technical treatise on the Tarot. The sequence of the 22 Trumps is explained as a formula of initiation.[4]

*CCXXXI*    Sum of the numbers $[0 + 1 + \ldots + 20 + 21]$ printed on the Tarot Trumps.[3]

## Liber CCCLXX

*Liber A'ash Vel Capricorni Pneumatici Sub Figurâ CCCLXX*
Contains the true secret of all practical magick.[1]

*The Book of Creation or of the Goat of the Spirit*
[A]nalyzes the nature of the creative magical force in man, explains how to awaken it, how to use it and indicates the general as well as the particular objects to be gained thereby.[4]

The Interpretation of this Book will be given to members of the Grade of Dominus Liminis on application, each to his Adeptus.[14]

*CCCLXX*    עץ Creation.[3]

## LIBER CD

*Liber Tᴀᴜ Vel Kabbalæ Trium Literarum Sub Figurâ CD*
A graphic interpretation of the Tarot on the plane of initiation.[1]

*Liber CD* analyzes the Hebrew alphabet into seven triads, each of which forms a Trinity of sympathetic ideas relating respectively to the Three Orders comprised in the A.'.A.'.. It is really an attempt to find a Periodic Law in the system.[4]

This analysis may be checked by adding the columns vertically, 69, 81, 93, 114, 135, 246, 357. Dividing by 3 we get 23, 27, 31, 38, 45, 82, 119, which in the *Sepher Sephiroth* mean respectively Life, Purity, Negation, «38 × 11 = 418,» Innocent, Formation, Prayer, Weeping. The analogies are obvious.[15]

CD          From the large Tau ת in the diagram.[3]

## LIBER DCCCXIII

*Vel Ararita Sub Figurâ DLXX*
This book is an account of the Hexagram and the method of reducing it to the Unity, and Beyond.[1]

This book describes in magical language a very secret process of Initiation.[2]

ARARITA (—a name of God, which is a Notariqon of the sentence: «One is His beginning; One is his Individuality; His Permutation One.») The use of this Name and Formula is to equate and identify every idea with its opposite; thus being released from the obsession of thinking any one of them as «true» (and therefore binding); one can withdraw oneself from the whole sphere of the Ruach. [ . . . ] Contrast each verse of Cap. I with the corresponding verse of Cap. II for the first of these methods. Thus in Cap. III (still verse by verse correspondence) the Quintessence of the ideas is extracted; and in Cap. IV they are withdrawn each one into the one beyond it. In Cap. V they have disappeared into the Method itself. In Cap. VI they reappear in the Form appointed by the Will of the Adept. Lastly, in Cap. VII they are dissolved, one into the next until all finally disappear in the Fire Qadosh, the Quintessence of Reality.[16]

The full knowledge of the interpretation of this book is concealed from all.

The Philosophus must nevertheless acquire a copy and thoroughly acquaint himself with the contents. He must commit one chapter to memory.[5]

*DCCCXIII*       See *Sepher Sephiroth.*[3]
*DLXX*[3]

# NOTES

1. Crowley, «A Syllabus of the Official Instructions of A.˙.A.˙. Hitherto Published», *The Equinox* I (10), 1913 (reprinted York Beach, ME: Weiser, 1972), pp. 43–47.
2. Crowley, «Præmonstrance of A.˙.A.˙.» and «Curriculum of A.˙.A.˙.», *The Equinox* III (1), 1919, pp. 11–38.
3. Crowley, «Syllabus», pp. 53–56.
4. Crowley, *The Confessions of Aleister Crowley*, (London: Cape, 1969), pp. 673–4.
5. Θελημα (London: privately printed, 1909), 3 vols. These notes are unique to this edition.
6. Crowley, *Preliminary Analysis of Liber LXV*, I:1; *cf.* Appendix C *infra* for bibliographic references.
7. Crowley, *The Equinox of the Gods* (London: O.T.O., 1936), p. 134.
8. *The Confessions of Aleister Crowley*, p. 399.
9. *Ibid.*, p. 396.
10. *Ibid.*, p. 398.
11. Crowley, *The Equinox of the Gods*, cover/title page to *Liber XXXI*.
12. *Ibid.*, pp. 104–5.
13. Crowley, «Index of Volume One», *The Equinox* I (10), 1913, p. 239.
14. Crowley, colophon to *Liber CCCLXX*, *The Equinox* I (6), p. 39.
15. Crowley, commentary to *Liber CD*, *The Equinox* I (7), p. 77.
16. Crowley, *Liber XXX Ærum Vel Sæculi Sub Figurâ CDXVIII* [...] *The Vision and the Voice*, with a Commentary by The Master Therion (Barstow, Calif.: Thelema Publishing Co., 1952), p. 43n.

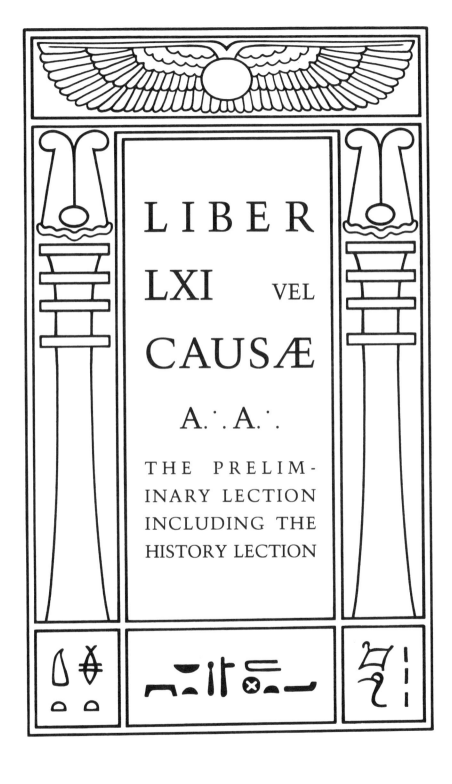

# LIBER

## LXI VEL

# CAUSÆ

A∴A∴

THE PRELIM-
INARY LECTION
INCLUDING THE
HISTORY LECTION

A∴A∴
Publication in Class D.

# THE PRELIMINARY LECTION

In the Name of the Initiator, Amen.

1. In the beginning was Initiation. The flesh profiteth nothing; the mind profiteth nothing; that which is unknown to you and above these, while firmly based upon their equilibrium, giveth life.

2. In all systems of religion is to be found a system of Initiation, which may be defined as the process by which a man comes to learn that unknown Crown.

3. Though none can communicate either the knowledge or the power to achieve this, which we may call the Great Work, it is yet possible for initiates to guide others.

4. Every man must overcome his own obstacles, expose his own illusions. Yet others may assist him to do both, and they may enable him altogether to avoid many of the false paths, leading no whither, which tempt the weary feet of the uninitiated pilgrim. They can further insure that he is duly tried and tested, for there are many who think themselves to be Masters who have not even begun to tread the Way of Service that leads thereto.

5. Now the Great Work is one, and the Initiation is one, and the Reward is one, however diverse are the symbols wherein the Unutterable is clothed.

6. Hear then the history of the system which this lection gives you the opportunity of investigating.

   Listen, we pray you, with attention: for once only does the Great Order knock at any one door.

Whosoever knows any member of that Order as such, can never know another, until he too has attained to mastery.

Here, therefore, we pause, that you may thoroughly search yourself, and consider if you are yet fitted to take an irrevocable step.

For the reading of that which follows is Recorded.

# THE HISTORY LECTION

7. Some years ago a number of cipher MSS. were discovered and deciphered by certain students. They attracted much attention, as they purported to derive from the Rosicrucians. You will readily understand that the genuineness of the claim matters no whit, such literature being judged by itself, not by its reputed sources.

8. Among the MSS. was one which gave the address of a certain person in Germany, who is known to us as S.D.A. Those who discovered the ciphers wrote to S.D.A., and in accordance with instructions received, an Order was founded which worked in a semi-secret manner.

9. After some time S.D.A. died: further requests for help were met with a prompt refusal from the colleagues of S.D.A. It was written by one of them that S.D.A.'s scheme had always been regarded with disapproval. But since the absolute rule of the adepts is never to interfere with the judgment of any other person whomsoever— how much more, then, one of themselves, and that one most highly revered!—they had refrained from active opposition. The adept who wrote this added that the Order had already quite enough knowledge to enable it or its members to formulate a magical link with the adepts.

10. Shortly after this, one called S.R.M.D. announced that he had formulated such a link, and that himself and two

others were to govern the Order. New and revised rituals were issued, and fresh knowledge poured out in streams.

11. We must pass over the unhappy juggleries which characterized the next period. It has throughout proved impossible to elucidate the complex facts.

    We content ourselves, then, with observing that the death of one of his two colleagues, and the weakness of the other, secured to S.R.M.D. the sole authority. The rituals were elaborated, though scholarly enough, into verbose and pretentious nonsense: the knowledge proved worthless, even where it was correct: for it is in vain that pearls, be they never so clear and precious, are given to the swine.

    The ordeals were turned into contempt, it being impossible for any one to fail therein. Unsuitable candidates were admitted for no better reason than that of their worldly prosperity.

    In short, the Order failed to initiate.

12. Scandal arose and with it schism.

13. In 1900 one P., a brother, instituted a rigorous test of S.R.M.D. on the one side and the Order on the other.

14. He discovered that S.R.M.D., though a scholar of some ability and a magician of remarkable powers, had never attained complete initiation: and further had fallen from his original place, he having imprudently attracted to himself forces of evil too great and terrible for him to withstand.

    The claim of the Order that the true adepts were in charge of it was definitely disproved.

15. In the Order, with two certain exceptions and two doubtful ones, he found no persons prepared for initiation of any sort.

INTRODUCTION xliii

16. He thereupon by his subtle wisdom destroyed both the Order and its chief.

17. Being himself no perfect adept, he was driven of the Spirit into the Wilderness, where he abode for six years, studying by the light of reason the sacred books and secret systems of initiation of all countries and ages.

18. Finally, there was given unto him a certain exalted grade whereby a man becomes master of knowledge and intelligence, and no more their slave. He perceived the inadequacy of science, philosophy, and religion; and exposed the self-contradictory nature of the thinking faculty.

19. Returning to England, he laid his achievements humbly at the feet of a certain adept D.D.S., who welcomed him brotherly and admitted his title to the grade which he had so hardly won.

20. Thereupon these two adepts conferred together, saying: May it not be written that the tribulations shall be shortened? Wherefore they resolved to establish a new Order which should be free from the errors and deceits of the former one.

21. Without Authority they could not do this, exalted as their rank was among adepts. They resolved to prepare all things, great and small, against that day when such Authority should be received by them, since they knew not where to seek for higher adepts than themselves, but knew that the true way to attract the notice of such was to equilibrate the symbols. The temple must be builded before the God can indwell it.

22. Therefore by the order of D.D.S. did P. prepare all things by his arcane science and wisdom, choosing only those symbols which were common to all systems, and rigorously rejecting all names and words which might

be supposed to imply any religious or metaphysical theory. To do this utterly was found impossible, since all language has a history, and the use (for example) of the word « spirit » implies the Scholastic Philosophy and the Hindu and Taoist theories concerning the breath of man. So was it difficult to avoid implication of some undesirable bias by using the words « order,» « circle,» « chapter,» « society,» « brotherhood,» or any other to designate the body of initiates.

23. Deliberately, therefore, did he take refuge in vagueness. Not to veil the truth to the Neophyte, but to warn him against valuing non-essentials. Should therefore the candidate hear the name of any God, let him not rashly assume that it refers to any known God, save only the God known to himself. Or should the ritual speak in terms (however vague) which seem to imply Egyptian, Taoist, Buddhist, Indian, Persian, Greek, Judaic, Christian, or Moslem philosophy, let him reflect that this is a defect of language; the literary limitation and not the spiritual prejudice of the man P.

24. Especially let him guard against the finding of definite sectarian symbols in the teaching of his master, and the reasoning from the known to the unknown which assuredly will tempt him.

We labour earnestly, dear brother, that you may never be led away to perish upon this point; for thereon have many holy and just men been wrecked. By this have all the visible systems lost the essence of wisdom.

We have sought to reveal the Arcanum; we have only profaned it.

25. Now when P. had thus with bitter toil prepared all things under the guidance of D.D.S. (even as the hand writes, while the conscious brain, though ignorant of the detailed movements, applauds or disapproves the

finished work) there was a certain time of repose, as the earth lieth fallow.

26. Meanwhile these adepts busied themselves intently with the Great Work.

27. In the fullness of time, even as a blossoming tree that beareth fruit in its season, all these pains were ended, and these adepts and their companions obtained the reward which they had sought—they were to be admitted to the Eternal and Invisible Order that hath no name among men.

28. They therefore who had with smiling faces abandoned their homes, their possessions, their wives, their children, in order to perform the Great Work, could with steady calm and firm correctness abandon the Great Work itself: for this is the last and greatest projection of the alchemist.

29. Also one V.V.V.V.V. arose, an exalted adept of the rank of Master of the Temple (or this much He disclosed to the Exempt Adepts) and His utterance is enshrined in the Sacred Writings.

30. Such are Liber Legis, Liber Cordis Cincti Serpente, Liber Liberi vel Lapidis Lazuli and such others whose existence may one day be divulged unto you. Beware lest you interpret them either in the Light or in the darkness, for only in L.V.X. may they be understood.

31. Also He conferred upon D.D.S., O.M., and another, the Authority of the Triad, who in turn have delegated it unto others, and they yet again, so that the Body of Initiates may be perfect, even from the Crown unto the Kingdom and beyond.

32. For Perfection abideth not in the Pinnacles, or in the Foundations, but in the ordered Harmony of one with all.

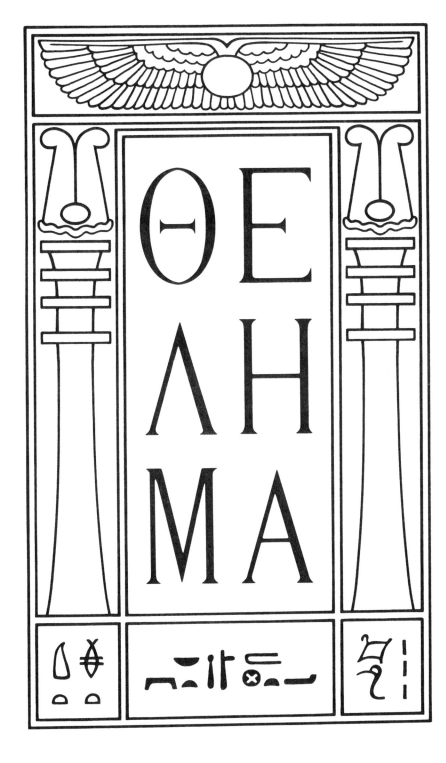

# LIBER

# B
VEL
# MAGI

SUB FIGURÂ

# I

A∴A∴
Publication in Class A.

00. One is the Magus: twain His forces: four His weapons. These are the Seven Spirits of Unrighteousness; seven vultures of evil. Thus is the art and craft of the Magus but glamour. How shall He destroy Himself?

0. Yet the Magus hath power upon the Mother both directly and through Love. And the Magus is Love, and bindeth together That and This in His Conjuration.

1. In the beginning doth the Magus speak Truth, and send forth Illusion and Falsehood to enslave the soul. Yet therein is the Mystery of Redemption.

2. By His Wisdom made He the Worlds; the Word that is God is none other than He.

3. How then shall He end His speech with Silence? For He is Speech.

4. He is the First and the Last. How shall He cease to number Himself?

5. By a Magus is this writing made known through the mind of a Magister. The one uttereth clearly, and the other understandeth; yet the Word is falsehood, and the Understanding darkness. And this saying is Of All Truth.

6. Nevertheless it is written; for there be times of darkness, and this as a lamp therein.

7. With the Wand createth He.

8. With the Cup preserveth He.

9. With the Dagger destroyeth He.

10. With the Coin redeemeth He.

11. His weapons fulfil the wheel; and on What Axle that turneth is not known unto Him.

12. From all these actions must He cease before the curse of His Grade is uplifted from Him. Before He attain to That which existeth without Form.

13. And if at this time He be manifested upon earth as a Man, and therefore is this present writing, let this be His method, that the curse of His grade, and the burden of His attainment, be uplifted from Him.

14. Let Him beware of abstinence from action. For the curse of His grade is that He must speak Truth, that the Falsehood thereof may enslave the souls of men. Let Him then utter that without Fear, that the Law may be fulfilled. And according to His Original Nature will that law be shapen, so that one may declare gentleness and quietness, being an Hindu; and another fierceness and servility, being a Jew; and yet another ardour and manliness, being an Arab. Yet this matter toucheth the mystery of Incarnation, and is not here to be declared.

15. Now the grade of a Magister teacheth the Mystery of Sorrow, and the grade of a Magus the Mystery of Change, and the grade of Ipsissimus the Mystery of Selflessness, which is called also the Mystery of Pan.

16. Let the Magus then contemplate each in turn, raising it to the ultimate power of Infinity. Wherein Sorrow is Joy, and Change is Stability, and Selflessness is Self. For the interplay of the parts hath no action upon the whole. And this contemplation shall be performed not by simple meditation—how much less then by reason? but by the method which shall have been given unto Him in His initiation to the Grade.

17. Following which method, it shall be easy for Him to combine that trinity from its elements, and further to combine Sat-Chit-Ananda, and Light, Love, Life, three

by three into nine that are one, in which meditation success shall be That which was first adumbrated to Him in the grade of Practicus (which reflecteth Mercury into the lowest world) in Liber XXVII, «Here is Nothing under its three Forms.»

18. And this is the Opening of the Grade of Ipsissimus, and by the Buddhists it is called the trance Nerodha-Samapatti.

19. And woe, woe, woe, yea woe, and again woe, woe, woe unto seven times be His that preacheth not His law to men!

20. And woe also be unto Him that refuseth the curse of the grade of a Magus, and the burden of the Attainment thereof.

21. And in the word CHAOS let the Book be sealed; yea, let the Book be sealed.

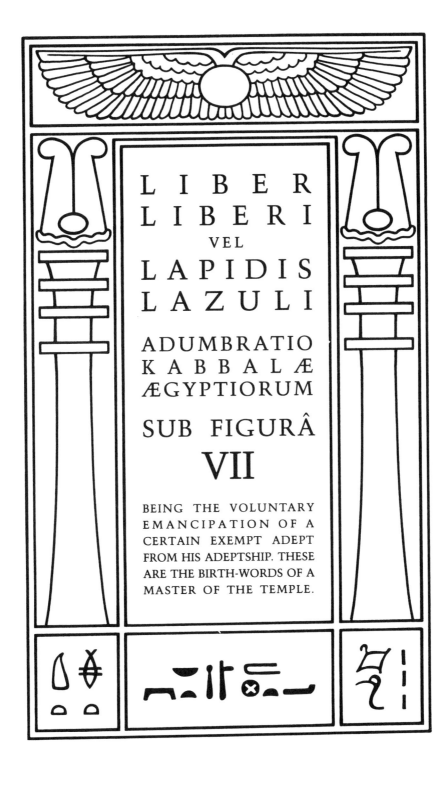

# LIBER LIBERI
VEL
## LAPIDIS LAZULI

ADUMBRATIO
KABBALÆ
ÆGYPTIORUM

SUB FIGURÂ
# VII

BEING THE VOLUNTARY
EMANCIPATION OF A
CERTAIN EXEMPT ADEPT
FROM HIS ADEPTSHIP. THESE
ARE THE BIRTH-WORDS OF A
MASTER OF THE TEMPLE.

A∴A∴
Publication in Class A.

# PROLOGUE OF THE UNBORN

1. Into my loneliness comes—
2. The sound of a flute in dim groves that haunt the uttermost hills.
3. Even from the brave river they reach to the edge of the wilderness.
4. And I behold Pan.
5. The snows are eternal above, above—
6. And their perfume smokes upward into the nostrils of the stars.
7. But what have I to do with these?
8. To me only the distant flute, the abiding vision of Pan.
9. On all sides Pan to the eye, to the ear;
10. The perfume of Pan pervading, the taste of him utterly filling my mouth, so that the tongue breaks forth into a weird and monstrous speech.
11. The embrace of him intense on every centre of pain and pleasure.
12. The sixth interior sense aflame with the inmost self of Him,
13. Myself flung down the precipice of being
14. Even to the abyss, annihilation.
15. An end to loneliness, as to all.
16. Pan! Pan! Io Pan! Io Pan!

# I

1. My God, how I love Thee!
2. With the vehement appetite of a beast I hunt Thee through the Universe.
3. Thou art standing as it were upon a pinnacle at the edge of some fortified city. I am a white bird, and perch upon Thee.
4. Thou art My Lover: I see Thee as a nymph with her white limbs stretched by the spring.
5. She lies upon the moss; there is none other but she:
6. Art Thou not Pan?
7. I am He. Speak not, O my God! Let the work be accomplished in silence.
8. Let my cry of pain be crystallized into a little white fawn to run away into the forest!
9. Thou art a centaur, O my God, from the violet-blossoms that crown Thee to the hoofs of the horse.
10. Thou art harder than tempered steel; there is no diamond beside Thee.
11. Did I not yield this body and soul?
12. I woo thee with a dagger drawn across my throat.
13. Let the spout of blood quench Thy blood-thirst, O my God!
14. Thou art a little white rabbit in the burrow Night.
15. I am greater than the fox and the hole.
16. Give me Thy kisses, O Lord God!
17. The lightning came and licked up the little flock of sheep.

18. There is a tongue and a flame; I see that trident walking over the sea.

19. A phœnix hath it for its head; below are two prongs. They spear the wicked.

20. I will spear Thee, O Thou little grey god, unless Thou beware!

21. From the grey to the gold; from the gold to that which is beyond the gold of Ophir.

22. My God! but I love Thee!

23. Why hast Thou whispered so ambiguous things? Wast Thou afraid, O goat-hoofed One, O horned One, O pillar of lightning?

24. From the lightning fall pearls; from the pearls black specks of nothing.

25. I based all on one, one on naught.

26. Afloat in the æther, O my God, my God!

27. O Thou great hooded sun of glory, cut off these eyelids!

28. Nature shall die out; she hideth me, closing mine eyelids with fear, she hideth me from My destruction, O Thou open eye.

29. O ever-weeping One!

30. Not Isis my mother, nor Osiris my self; but the incestuous Horus given over to Typhon, so may I be!

31. There thought; and thought is evil.

32. Pan! Pan! Io Pan! it is enough.

33. Fall not into death, O my soul! Think that death is the bed into which you are falling!

34. O how I love Thee, O my God! Especially is there a vehement parallel light from infinity, vilely diffracted in the haze of this mind.

35. I love Thee.
    I love Thee.
    I love Thee.

36. Thou art a beautiful thing whiter than a woman in the column of this vibration.

37. I shoot up vertically like an arrow, and become that Above.

38. But it is death, and the flame of the pyre.

39. Ascend in the flame of the pyre, O my soul! Thy God is like the cold emptiness of the utmost heaven, into which thou radiatest thy little light.

40. When Thou shall know me, O empty God, my flame shall utterly expire in Thy great N. O. X.

41. What shalt Thou be, my God, when I have ceased to love Thee?

42. A worm, a nothing, a niddering knave!

43. But Oh! I love Thee.

44. I have thrown a million flowers from the basket of the Beyond at Thy feet, I have anointed Thee and Thy Staff with oil and blood and kisses.

45. I have kindled Thy marble into life—ay! into death.

46. I have been smitten with the reek of Thy mouth, that drinketh never wine but life.

47. How the dew of the Universe whitens the lips!

48. Ah! trickling flow of the stars of the mother Supernal, begone!

49. I Am She that should come, the Virgin of all men.

50. I am a boy before Thee, O Thou satyr God.

51. Thou wilt inflict the punishment of pleasure—Now! Now! Now!

52. Io Pan! Io Pan! I love Thee. I love Thee.

53. O my God, spare me!

54. Now!
    It is done! Death.

55. I cried aloud the word—and it was a mighty spell to bind the Invisible, an enchantment to unbind the bound; yea, to unbind the bound.

# II

1. O my God! use Thou me again, alway.  For ever!  For ever!

2. That which came fire from Thee cometh water from me; let therefore Thy Spirit lay hold on me, so that my right hand loose the lightning.

3. Travelling through space, I saw the onrush of two galaxies, butting each other and goring like bulls upon earth.  I was afraid.

4. Thus they ceased fight, and turned upon me, and I was sorely crushed and torn.

5. I had rather have been trampled by the World-Elephant.

6. O my God!  Thou art my little pet tortoise!

7. Yet Thou sustainest the World-Elephant.

8. I creep under Thy carapace, like a lover into the bed of his beautiful; I creep in, and sit in Thine heart, as cubby and cosy as may be.

9. Thou shelterest me, that I hear not the trumpeting of that World-Elephant.

10. Thou art not worth an obol in the agora; yet Thou art not to be bought at the ransom of the whole Universe.

11. Thou art like a beautiful Nubian slave leaning her naked purple against the green pillars of marble that are above the bath.

12. Wine jets from her black nipples.

13. I drank wine awhile agone in the house of Pertinax. The cup-boy favoured me, and gave me of the right sweet Chian.

14. There was a Doric boy, skilled in feats of strength, an athlete. The full moon fled away angrily down the wrack.

    Ah! but we laughed.
15. I was pernicious drunk, O my God! Yet Pertinax brought me to the bridal.
16. I had a crown of thorns for all my dower.
17. Thou art like a goat's horn from Astor, O Thou God of mine, gnarl'd and crook'd and devilish strong.
18. Colder than all the ice of all the glaciers of the Naked Mountain was the wine it poured for me.
19. A wild country and a waning moon.

    Clouds scudding over the sky.

    A circuit of pines, and of tall yews beyond. Thou in the midst!
20. O all ye toads and cats, rejoice! Ye slimy things, come hither!
21. Dance, dance to the Lord our God!
22. He is he! He is he! He is he!
23. Why should I go on?
24. Why? Why? comes the sudden cackle of a million imps of hell.
25. And the laughter runs.
26. But sickens not the Universe; but shakes not the stars.
27. God! how I love Thee!
28. I am walking in an asylum; all the men and women about me are insane.
29. Oh madness! madness! madness! desirable art thou!
30. But I love Thee, O God!
31. These men and women rave and howl; they froth out folly.
32. I begin to be afraid. I have no check; I am alone. Alone. Alone.
33. Think, O God, how I am happy in Thy love.
34. O marble Pan! O false leering face! I love Thy dark

kisses, bloody and stinking! O marble Pan! Thy kisses are like sunlight on the blue Ægean; their blood is the blood of the sunset over Athens; their stink is like a garden of Roses of Macedonia.

35. I dreamt of sunset and roses and vines; Thou wast there, O my God, Thou didst habit Thyself as an Athenian courtesan, and I loved Thee.

36. Thou art no dream, O Thou too beautiful alike for sleep and waking!

37. I disperse the insane folk of the earth; I walk alone with my little puppets in the garden.

38. I am Gargantuan great; yon galaxy is but the smoke-ring of mine incense.

39. Burn Thou strange herbs, O God!

40. Brew me a magic liquor, boys, with your glances!

41. The very soul is drunken.

42. Thou art drunken, O my God, upon my kisses.

43. The Universe reels; Thou hast looked upon it.

44. Twice, and all is done.

45. Come, O my God, and let us embrace!

46. Lazily, hungrily, ardently, patiently; so will I work.

47. There shall be an End.

48. O God! O God!

49. I am a fool to love Thee; Thou art cruel, Thou withholdest Thyself.

50. Come to me now! I love Thee! I love Thee!

51. O my darling, my darling—Kiss me! Kiss me! Ah! but again.

52. Sleep, take me! Death, take me! This life is too full; it pains, it slays, it suffices.

53. Let me go back into the world; yea, back into the world.

# III

1. I was the priest of Ammon-Ra in the temple of Ammon-Ra at Thebai.
2. But Bacchus came singing with his troops of vine-clad girls, of girls in dark mantles; and Bacchus in the midst like a fawn!
3. God! how I ran out in my rage and scattered the chorus!
4. But in my temple stood Bacchus as the priest of Ammon-Ra.
5. Therefore I went wildly with the girls into Abyssinia; and there we abode and rejoiced.
6. Exceedingly; yea, in good sooth!
7. I will eat the ripe and the unripe fruit for the glory of Bacchus.
8. Terraces of ilex, and tiers of onyx and opal and sardonyx leading up to the cool green porch of malachite.
9. Within is a crystal shell, shaped like an oyster—O glory of Priapus! O beatitude of the Great Goddess!
10. Therein is a pearl.
11. O Pearl! thou hast come from the majesty of dread Ammon-Ra.
12. Then I the priest beheld a steady glitter in the heart of the pearl.
13. So bright we could not look! But behold! a blood-red rose upon a rood of glowing gold!
14. So I adored the God. Bacchus! thou art the lover of my God!

17

15. I who was priest of Ammon-Ra, who saw the Nile flow by for many moons, for many, many moons, am the young fawn of the grey land.

16. I will set up my dance in your conventicles, and my secret loves shall be sweet among you.

17. Thou shalt have a lover among the lords of the grey land.

18. This shall he bring unto thee, without which all is in vain; a man's life spilt for thy love upon Mine Altars.

19. Amen.

20. Let it be soon, O God, my God! I ache for Thee, I wander very lonely among the mad folk, in the grey land of desolation.

21. Thou shalt set up the abominable lonely Thing of wickedness. Oh joy! to lay that corner-stone!

22. It shall stand erect upon the high mountain; only my God shall commune with it.

23. I will build it of a single ruby; it shall be seen from afar off.

24. Come! let us irritate the vessels of the earth: they shall distil strange wine.

25. It grows under my hand: it shall cover the whole heaven.

26. Thou art behind me: I scream with a mad joy.

27. Then said Ithuriel the strong; let Us also worship this invisible marvel!

28. So did they, and the archangels swept over the heaven.

29. Strange and mystic, like a yellow priest invoking mighty flights of great grey birds from the North, so do I stand and invoke Thee!

30. Let them obscure not the sun with their wings and their clamour!

31. Take away form and its following!

32. I am still.

33. Thou art like an osprey among the rice, I am the great red pelican in the sunset waters.

34. I am like a black eunuch; and Thou art the scimitar. I smite off the head of the light one, the breaker of bread and salt.

35. Yea! I smite—and the blood makes as it were a sunset on the lapis lazuli of the King's Bedchamber.

36. I smite. The whole world is broken up into a mighty wind, and a voice cries aloud in a tongue that men cannot speak.

37. I know that awful sound of primal joy; let us follow on the wings of the gale even unto the holy house of Hathor; let us offer the five jewels of the cow upon her altar!

38. Again the inhuman voice!

39. I rear my Titan bulk into the teeth of the gale, and I smite and prevail, and swing me out over the sea.

40. There is a strange pale God, a god of pain and deadly wickedness.

41. My own soul bites into itself, like a scorpion ringed with fire.

42. That pallid God with face averted, that God of subtlety and laughter, that young Doric God, him will I serve.

43. For the end thereof is torment unspeakable.

44. Better the loneliness of the great grey sea!

45. But ill befall the folk of the grey land, my God!

46. Let me smother them with my roses!

47. Oh Thou delicious God, smile sinister!

48. I pluck Thee, O my God, like a purple plum upon a sunny tree. How Thou dost melt in my mouth, Thou consecrated sugar of the Stars!

49. The world is all grey before mine eyes; it is like an old worn wine-skin.

50. All the wine of it is on these lips.

51. Thou hast begotten me upon a marble Statue, O my God!

52. The body is icy cold with the coldness of a million moons; it is harder than the adamant of eternity. How shall I come forth into the light?

53. Thou art He, O God! O my darling! my child! my plaything! Thou art like a cluster of maidens, like a multitude of swans upon the lake.

54. I feel the essence of softness.

55. I am hard and strong and male; but come Thou! I shall be soft and weak and feminine.

56. Thou shalt crush me in the wine-press of Thy love. My blood shall stain Thy fiery feet with litanies of Love in Anguish.

57. There shall be a new flower in the fields, a new vintage in the vineyards.

58. The bees shall gather a new honey; the poets shall sing a new song.

59. I shall gain the Pain of the Goat for my prize; and the God that sitteth upon the shoulders of Time shall drowse.

60. Then shall all this which is written be accomplished: yea, it shall be accomplished.

# IV

1. I am like a maiden bathing in a clear pool of fresh water.
2. O my God! I see Thee dark and desirable, rising through the water as a golden smoke.
3. Thou art altogether golden, the hair and the eyebrows and the brilliant face; even into the finger-tips and toe-tips Thou art one rosy dream of gold.
4. Deep into Thine eyes that are golden my soul leaps, like an archangel menacing the sun.
5. My sword passes through and through Thee; crystalline moons ooze out of Thy beautiful body that is hidden behind the ovals of Thine eyes.
6. Deeper, ever deeper. I fall, even as the whole Universe falls down the abyss of Years.
7. For Eternity calls; the Overworld calls; the world of the Word is awaiting us.
8. Be done with speech, O God! Fasten the fangs of the hound Eternity in this my throat!
9. I am like a wounded bird flapping in circles.
10. Who knows where I shall fall?
11. O blessèd One! O God! O my devourer!
12. Let me fall, fall down, fall away, afar, alone!
13. Let me fall!
14. Nor is there any rest, Sweet Heart, save in the cradle of royal Bacchus, the thigh of the most Holy One.
15. There rest, under the canopy of night.
16. Uranus chid Eros; Marsyas chid Olympas; I chid my beautiful lover with his sunray mane; shall I not sing?

17. Shall not mine incantations bring around me the wonderful company of the wood-gods, their bodies glistening with the ointment of moonlight and honey and myrrh?

18. Worshipful are ye, O my lovers; let us forward to the dimmest hollow!

19. There we will feast upon mandrake and upon moly!

20. There the lovely One shall spread us His holy banquet. In the brown cakes of corn we shall taste the food of the world, and be strong.

21. In the ruddy and awful cup of death we shall drink the blood of the world, and be drunken!

22. Ohé! the song to Iao, the song to Iao!

23. Come, let us sing to thee, Iacchus invisible, Iacchus triumphant, Iacchus indicible!

24. Iacchus, O Iacchus, O Iacchus, be near us!

25. Then was the countenance of all time darkened, and the true light shone forth.

26. There was also a certain cry in an unknown tongue, whose stridency troubled the still waters of my soul, so that my mind and my body were healed of their disease, self-knowledge.

27. Yea, an angel troubled the waters.

28. This was the cry of Him: IIIOOShBTh-IO-IIIIAMAMThIBI-II.

29. Nor did I sing this for a thousand times a night for a thousand nights before Thou camest, O my flaming God, and pierced me with Thy spear. Thy scarlet robe unfolded the whole heavens, so that the Gods said: All is burning: it is the end.

30. Also Thou didst set Thy lips to the wound and suck out a million eggs. And Thy mother sat upon them, and lo! stars and stars and ultimate Things whereof stars are the atoms.

31. Then I perceived Thee, O my God, sitting like a white cat upon the trellis-work of the arbour; and the hum of the spinning worlds was but Thy pleasure.

32. O white cat, the sparks fly from Thy fur! Thou dost crackle with splitting the worlds.

33. I have seen more of Thee in the white cat than I saw in the Vision of Æons.

34. In the boat of Ra did I travel, but I never found upon the visible Universe any being like unto Thee!

35. Thou wast like a winged white horse, and I raced Thee through eternity against the Lord of the Gods.

36. So still we race!

37. Thou wast like a flake of snow falling in the pine-clad woods.

38. In a moment Thou wast lost in a wilderness of the like and the unlike.

39. But I beheld the beautiful God at the back of the blizzard—and Thou wast He!

40. Also I read in a great Book.

41. On ancient skin was written in letters of gold: Verbum fit Verbum.

42. Also Vitriol and the hierophant's name
V.V.V.V.V.

43. All this wheeled in fire, in star-fire, rare and far and utterly lonely—even as Thou and I, O desolate soul my God!

44. Yea, and the writing

It is well.

This is the voice which shook the earth.

45. Eight times he cried aloud, and by eight and by eight shall I count Thy favours, Oh Thou Elevenfold God 418!

46. Yea, and by many more; by the ten in the twenty-two directions; even as the perpendicular of the Pyramid— so shall Thy favours be.

47. If I number them, they are One.

48. Excellent is Thy love, Oh Lord! Thou art revealed by the darkness, and he who gropeth in the horror of the groves shall haply catch Thee, even as a snake that seizeth on a little singing-bird.

49. I have caught Thee, O my soft thrush; I am like a hawk of mother-of-emerald; I catch Thee by instinct, though my eyes fail from Thy glory.

50. Yet they are but foolish folk yonder. I see them on the yellow sand, all clad in Tyrian purple.

51. They draw their shining God unto the land in nets; they build a fire to the Lord of Fire, and cry unhallowed words, even the dreadful curse Amri maratza, maratza, atman deona lastadza maratza maritza—marán!

52. Then do they cook the shining god, and gulp him whole.

53. These are evil folk, O beautiful boy! let us pass on to the Otherworld.

54. Let us make ourselves into a pleasant bait, into a seductive shape!

55. I will be like a splendid naked woman with ivory breasts and golden nipples; my whole body shall be like the milk of the stars. I will be lustrous and Greek, a courtesan of Delos, of the unstable Isle.

56. Thou shalt be like a little red worm on a hook.

57. But thou and I will catch our fish alike.

58. Then wilt thou be a shining fish with golden back and

silver belly: I will be like a violent beautiful man, stronger than two score bulls, a man of the West bearing a great sack of precious jewels upon a staff that is greater than the axis of the all.

59. And the fish shall be sacrificed to Thee and the strong man crucified for Me, and Thou and I will kiss, and atone for the wrong of the Beginning; yea, for the wrong of the beginning.

# V

1. O my beautiful God! I swim in Thy heart like a trout in the mountain torrent.
2. I leap from pool to pool in my joy; I am goodly with brown and gold and silver.
3. Why, I am lovelier than the russet autumn woods at the first snowfall.
4. And the crystal cave of my thought is lovelier than I.
5. Only one fish-hook can draw me out; it is a woman kneeling by the bank of the stream. It is she that pours the bright dew over herself, and into the sand so that the river gushes forth.
6. There is a bird on yonder myrtle; only the song of that bird can draw me out of the pool of Thy heart, O my God!
7. Who is this Neapolitan boy that laughs in his happiness? His lover is the mighty crater of the Mountain of Fire. I saw his charred limbs borne down the slopes in a stealthy tongue of liquid stone.
8. And Oh! the chirp of the cicada!
9. I remember the days when I was cacique in Mexico.
10. O my God, wast Thou then as now my beautiful lover?
11. Was my boyhood then as now Thy toy, Thy joy?
12. Verily, I remember those iron days.
13. I remember how we drenched the bitter lakes with our torrent of gold; how we sank the treasurable image in the crater of Citlaltepetl.

14. How the good flame lifted us even unto the lowlands, setting us down in the impenetrable forest.
15. Yea, Thou wast a strange scarlet bird with a bill of gold. I was Thy mate in the forests of the lowland; and ever we heard from afar the shrill chant of mutilated priests and the insane clamour of the Sacrifice of Maidens.
16. There was a weird winged God that told us of his wisdom.
17. We attained to be starry grains of gold dust in the sands of a slow river.
18. Yea, and that river was the river of space and time also.
19. We parted thence; ever to the smaller, ever to the greater, until now, O sweet God, we are ourselves, the same.
20. O God of mine, Thou art like a little white goat with lightning in his horns!
21. I love Thee, I love Thee.
22. Every breath, every word, every thought, every deed is an act of love with Thee.
23. The beat of my heart is the pendulum of love.
24. The songs of me are the soft sighs:
25. The thoughts of me are very rapture:
26. And my deeds are the myriads of Thy children, the stars and the atoms.
27. Let there be nothing!
28. Let all things drop into this ocean of love!
29. Be this devotion a potent spell to exorcise the demons of the Five!
30. Ah God, all is gone! Thou dost consummate Thy rapture. Falútli! Falútli!
31. There is a solemnity of the silence. There is no more voice at all.

32. So shall it be unto the end.  We who were dust shall never fall away into the dust.
33. So shall it be.
34. Then, O my God, the breath of the Garden of Spices. All these have a savour averse.
35. The cone is cut with an infinite ray; the curve of hyperbolic life springs into being.
36. Farther and farther we float; yet we are still.  It is the chain of systems that is falling away from us.
37. First falls the silly world; the world of the old grey land.
38. Falls it unthinkably far, with its sorrowful bearded face presiding over it; it fades to silence and woe.
39. We to silence and bliss, and the face is the laughing face of Eros.
40. Smiling we greet him with the secret signs.
41. He leads us into the Inverted Palace.
42. There is the Heart of Blood, a pyramid reaching its apex down beyond the Wrong of the Beginning.
43. Bury me unto Thy Glory, O beloved, O princely lover of this harlot maiden, within the Secretest Chamber of the Palace!
44. It is done quickly; yea, the seal is set upon the vault.
45. There is one that shall avail to open it.
46. Nor by memory, nor by imagination, nor by prayer, nor by fasting, nor by scourging, nor by drugs, nor by ritual, nor by meditation; only by passive love shall he avail.
47. He shall await the sword of the Beloved and bare his throat for the stroke.
48. Then shall his blood leap out and write me runes in the sky; yea, write me runes in the sky.

# VI

1. Thou wast a priestess, O my God, among the Druids; and we knew the powers of the oak.
2. We made us a temple of stones in the shape of the Universe, even as thou didst wear openly and I concealed.
3. There we performed many wonderful things by midnight.
4. By the waning moon did we work.
5. Over the plain came the atrocious cry of wolves.
6. We answered; we hunted with the pack.
7. We came even unto the new Chapel and Thou didst bear away the Holy Graal beneath Thy Druid vestments.
8. Secretly and by stealth did we drink of the informing sacrament.
9. Then a terrible disease seized upon the folk of the grey land; and we rejoiced.
10. O my God, disguise Thy glory!
11. Come as a thief, and let us steal away the Sacraments!
12. In our groves, in our cloistral cells, in our honeycomb of happiness, let us drink, let us drink!
13. It is the wine that tinges everything with the true tincture of infallible gold.
14. There are deep secrets in these songs. It is not enough to hear the bird; to enjoy song he must be the bird.
15. I am the bird, and Thou art my song, O my glorious galloping God!

16. Thou reinest in the stars; thou drivest the constellations seven abreast through the circus of Nothingness.

17. Thou Gladiator God!

18. I play upon mine harp; Thou fightest the beasts and the flames.

19. Thou takest Thy joy in the music, and I in the fighting.

20. Thou and I are beloved of the Emperor.

21. See! he has summoned us to the Imperial dais.
    The night falls; it is a great orgy of worship and bliss.

22. The night falls like a spangled cloak from the shoulders of a prince upon a slave.

23. He rises a free man!

24. Cast thou, O prophet, the cloak upon these slaves!

25. A great night, and scarce fires therein; but freedom for the slave that its glory shall encompass.

26. So also I went down into the great sad city.

27. There dead Messalina bartered her crown for poison from the dead Locusta; there stood Caligula, and smote the seas of forgetfulness.

28. Who wast Thou, O Cæsar, that Thou knewest God in an horse?

29. For lo! we beheld the White Horse of the Saxon engraven upon the earth; and we beheld the Horses of the Sea that flame about the old grey land, and the foam from their nostrils enlightens us!

30. Ah! but I love thee, God!

31. Thou art like a moon upon the ice-world.

32. Thou art like the dawn of the utmost snows upon the burnt-up flats of the tiger's land.

33. By silence and by speech do I worship Thee.

34. But all is in vain.

35. Only Thy silence and Thy speech that worship me avail.

36. Wail, O ye folk of the grey land, for we have drunk your wine, and left ye but the bitter dregs.
37. Yet from these we will distil ye a liquor beyond the nectar of the Gods.
38. There is value in our tincture for a world of Spice and gold.
39. For our red powder of projection is beyond all possibilities.
40. There are few men; there are enough.
41. We shall be full of cup-bearers, and the wine is not stinted.
42. O dear my God! what a feast Thou hast provided.
43. Behold the lights and the flowers and the maidens!
44. Taste of the wines and the cates and the splendid meats!
45. Breathe in the perfumes and the clouds of little gods like wood-nymphs that inhabit the nostrils!
46. Feel with your whole body the glorious smoothness of the marble coolth and the generous warmth of the sun and the slaves!
47. Let the Invisible inform all the devouring Light of its disruptive vigour!
48. Yea! all the world is split apart, as an old grey tree by the lightning!
49. Come, O ye gods, and let us feast.
50. Thou, O my darling, O my ceaseless Sparrow-God, my delight, my desire, my deceiver, come Thou and chirp at my right hand!
51. This was the tale of the memory of Al A'in the priest; yea, of Al A'in the priest.

# VII

1. By the burning of the incense was the Word revealed, and by the distant drug.
2. O meal and honey and oil! O beautiful flag of the moon, that she hangs out in the centre of bliss!
3. These loosen the swathings of the corpse; these unbind the feet of Osiris, so that the flaming God may rage through the firmament with his fantastic spear.
4. But of pure black marble is the sorry statue, and the changeless pain of the eyes is bitter to the blind.
5. We understand the rapture of that shaken marble, torn by the throes of the crowned child, the golden rod of the golden God.
6. We know why all is hidden in the stone, within the coffin, within the mighty sepulchre, and we too answer Olalám! Imál! Tutúlu! as it is written in the ancient book.
7. Three words of that book are as life to a new æon; no god has read the whole.
8. But Thou and I, O God, have written it page by page.
9. Ours is the elevenfold reading of the Elevenfold word.
10. These seven letters together make seven diverse words; each word is divine, and seven sentences are hidden therein.
11. Thou art the Word, O my darling, my lord, my master!
12. O come to me, mix the fire and the water, all shall dissolve.

13. I await Thee in sleeping, in waking. I invoke Thee no more; for Thou art in me, O Thou who hast made me a beautiful instrument tuned to Thy rapture.

14. Yet art Thou ever apart, even as I.

15. I remember a certain holy day in the dusk of the year, in the dusk of the Equinox of Osiris, when first I beheld Thee visibly; when first the dreadful issue was fought out; when the Ibis-headed One charmed away the strife.

16. I remember Thy first kiss, even as a maiden should. Nor in the dark byways was there another: Thy kisses abide.

17. There is none other beside Thee in the whole Universe of Love.

18. My God, I love Thee, O Thou goat with gilded horns!

19. Thou beautiful bull of Apis! Thou beautiful serpent of Apep! Thou beautiful child of the Pregnant Goddess!

20. Thou hast stirred in Thy sleep, O ancient sorrow of years! Thou hast raised Thine head to strike, and all is dissolved into the Abyss of Glory.

21. An end to the letters of the words! An end to the sevenfold speech.

22. Resolve me the wonder of it all into the figure of a gaunt swift camel striding over the sand.

23. Lonely is he, and abominable; yet hath he gained the crown.

24. Oh rejoice! rejoice!

25. My God! O my God! I am but a speck in the star-dust of ages; I am the Master of the Secret of Things.

26. I am the Revealer and the Preparer. Mine is the Sword—and the Mitre and the Wingèd Wand!

27. I am the Initiator and the Destroyer. Mine is the Globe—and the Bennu Bird and the Lotus of Isis my daughter!

28. I am the One beyond these all; and I bear the symbols of the mighty darkness.

29. There shall be a sigil as of a vast black brooding ocean of death and the central blaze of darkness, radiating its night upon all.

30. It shall swallow up that lesser darkness.

31. But in that profound who shall answer: What is?

32. Not I.

33. Not Thou, O God!

34. Come, let us no more reason together; let us enjoy! Let us be ourselves, silent, unique, apart.

35. O lonely woods of the world! In what recesses will ye hide our love?

36. The forest of the spears of the Most High is called Night, and Hades, and the Day of Wrath; but I am His captain, and I bear His cup.

37. Fear me not with my spearmen! They shall slay the demons with their petty prongs. Ye shall be free.

38. Ah, slaves! ye will not—ye know not how to will.

39. Yet the music of my spears shall be a song of freedom.

40. A great bird shall sweep from the Abyss of Joy, and bear ye away to be my cup-bearers.

41. Come, O my God, in one last rapture let us attain to the Union with the Many!

42. In the silence of Things, in the Night of Forces, beyond the accursèd domain of the Three, let us enjoy our love!

43. My darling! My darling! away, away beyond the Assembly and the Law and the Enlightenment unto an Anarchy of Solitude and Darkness!

44. For even thus must we veil the brilliance of our Self.

45. My darling! My darling!

46. O my God, but the love in Me bursts over the bonds of Space and Time; my love is spilt among them that love not love.

47. My wine is poured out for them that never tasted wine.

48. The fumes thereof shall intoxicate them and the vigour of my love shall breed mighty children from their maidens.

49. Yea! without draught, without embrace:—and the Voice answered Yea! these things shall be.

50. Then I sought a Word for Myself; nay, for myself.

51. And the Word came: O Thou! it is well. Heed naught! I love Thee! I love Thee!

52. Therefore had I faith unto the end of all; yea, unto the end of all.

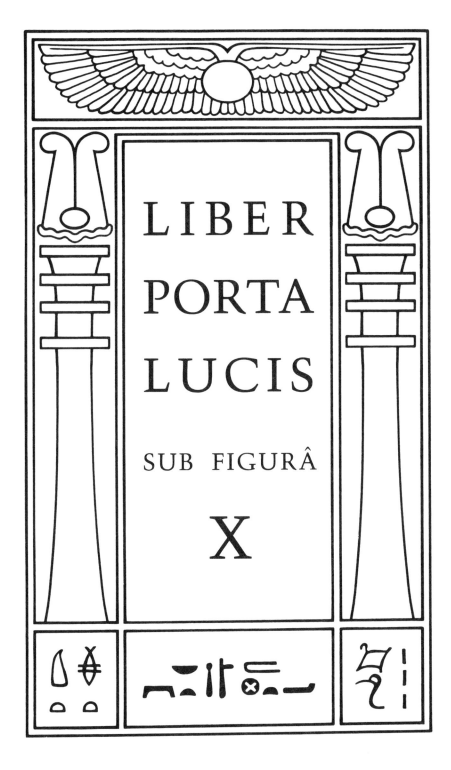

# LIBER PORTA LUCIS

## SUB FIGURÂ

## X

A∴A∴
Publication in Class A.

1. I behold a small dark orb, wheeling in an abyss of infinite space. It is minute among a myriad vast ones, dark amid a myriad bright ones.
2. I who comprehend in myself all the vast and the minute, all the bright and the dark, have mitigated the brilliance of mine unutterable splendour, sending forth V.V.V.V.V. as a ray of my light, as a messenger unto that small dark orb.
3. Then V.V.V.V.V. taketh up the word, and sayeth:
4. Men and women of the Earth, to you am I come from the Ages beyond the Ages, from the Space beyond your vision; and I bring to you these words.
5. But they heard him not, for they were not ready to receive them.
6. But certain men heard and understood, and through them shall this Knowledge be made known.
7. The least therefore of them, the servant of them all, writeth this book.
8. He writeth for them that are ready. Thus is it known if one be ready, if he be endowed with certain gifts, if he be fitted by birth, or by wealth, or by intelligence, or by some other manifest sign. And the servants of the master by his insight shall judge of these.
9. This Knowledge is not for all men; few indeed are called, but of these few many are chosen.
10. This is the nature of the Work.

11. First, there are many and diverse conditions of life upon this earth. In all of these is some seed of sorrow. Who can escape from sickness and from old age and from death?

12. We are come to save our fellows from these things. For there is a life intense with knowledge and extreme bliss which is untouched by any of them.

13. To this life we attain even here and now. The adepts, the servants of V.V.V.V.V., have attained thereunto.

14. It is impossible to tell you of the splendours of that to which they have attained.

    Little by little, as your eyes grow stronger, will we unveil to you the ineffable glory of the Path of the Adepts, and its nameless goal.

15. Even as a man ascending a steep mountain is lost to sight of his friends in the valley, so must the adept seem. They shall say: He is lost in the clouds. But he shall rejoice in the sunlight above them, and come to the eternal snows.

16. Or as a scholar may learn some secret language of the ancients, his friends shall say: « Look! he pretends to read this book. But it is unintelligible—it is non-sense. » Yet he delights in the Odyssey, while they read vain and vulgar things.

17. We shall bring you to Absolute Truth, Absolute Light, Absolute Bliss.

18. Many adepts throughout the ages have sought to do this; but their words have been perverted by their successors, and again and again the Veil has fallen upon the Holy of Holies.

19. To you who yet wander in the Court of the Profane we cannot yet reveal all; but you will easily understand that the religions of the world are but symbols and veils of the Absolute Truth. So also are the philosophies. To

the adept, seeing all these things from above, there seems nothing to choose between Buddha and Mohammed, between Atheism and Theism.

20. The many change and pass; the one remains. Even as wood and coal and iron burn up together in one great flame, if only that furnace be of transcendent heat; so in the alembic of this spiritual alchemy, if only the zelator blow sufficiently upon his furnace all the systems of earth are consumed in the One Knowledge.

21. Nevertheless, as a fire cannot be started with iron alone, in the beginning one system may be suited for one seeker, another for another.

22. We therefore who are without the chains of ignorance, look closely into the heart of the seeker and lead him by the path which is best suited to his nature unto the ultimate end of all things, the supreme realization, the Life which abideth in Light, yea, the Life which abideth in Light.

# LIBER TRIG-RAMM-ATON

## SUB FIGURÂ

# XXVII

BEING
THE BOOK OF THE
TRIGRAMS OF THE
MUTATIONS OF
THE TAO WITH THE
YIN AND THE YANG

A∴A∴
Publication in Class A.

Here is Nothing under its three forms. It is not, yet informeth all things.

Now cometh the glory of the Single One, as an imperfection and stain.

But by the Weak One the Mother was it equilibrated.

Also the purity was divided by Strength, the force of the Demiurge.

And the Cross was formulated in the Universe that as yet was not.

But now the Imperfection became manifest, presiding over the fading of perfection.

Also the Woman arose, and veiled the Upper Heaven with her body of stars.

Now then a giant arose, of terrible strength; and asserted the Spirit in a secret rite.

And the Master of the Temple balancing all things arose; his stature was above the Heaven and below Earth and Hell.

Against him the Brothers of the Left-hand Path, confusing the symbols. They concealed their horror [in this symbol]; for in truth they were

The master flamed forth as a star and set a guard of Water in every Abyss.

Also certain secret ones concealed the Light of Purity in themselves, protecting it from the Persecutions.

Likewise also did certain sons and daughters of Hermes and of Aphrodite, more openly

But the Enemy confused them. They pretended to conceal that Light, that they might betray it, and profane it.

Yet certain holy nuns concealed the secret in songs upon the lyre.

Now did the Horror of Time pervert all things, hiding the Purity with a loathsome thing, a thing unnameable.

Yea, and there arose sensualists upon the firmament, as a foul stain of storm upon the sky.

And the Black Brothers raised their heads; yea, they unveiled themselves without shame or fear.

Also there rose up a soul of filth and of weakness, and it corrupted all the rule of the Tao.

Then only was Heaven established to bear sway; for only in the lowest corruption is form manifest.

Also did Heaven manifest in violent light,

And in soft light.

Then were the waters gathered together from the heaven,

And a crust of earth concealed the core of flame.

Around the globe gathered the wide air,

And men began to light fires upon the earth.

Therefore was the end of it sorrow; yet in that sorrow a sixfold star of glory whereby they might see to return unto the stainless Abode; yea, unto the Stainless Abode.

# LIBER LXV

## LIBER CORDIS CINCTI SERPENTE

### SUB FIGURÂ

אדני

A∴A∴
Publication in Class A.

# I

1. I am the Heart; and the Snake is entwined
   About the invisible core of the mind.
   Rise, O my snake! It is now is the hour
   Of the hooded and holy ineffable flower.
   Rise, O my snake, into brilliance of bloom
   On the corpse of Osiris afloat in the tomb!
   O heart of my mother, my sister, mine own,
   Thou art given to Nile, to the terror Typhon!
   Ah me! but the glory of ravening storm
   Enswathes thee and wraps thee in frenzy of form.
   Be still, O my soul! that the spell may dissolve
   As the wands are upraised, and the æons revolve.
   Behold! in my beauty how joyous Thou art,
   O Snake that caresses the crown of mine heart!
   Behold! we are one, and the tempest of years
   Goes down to the dusk, and the Beetle appears.
   O Beetle! the drone of Thy dolorous note
   Be ever the trance of this tremulous throat!
   I await the awaking! The summons on high
   From the Lord Adonai, from the Lord Adonai!
2. Adonai spake unto V.V.V.V.V., saying: There must
   ever be division in the word.
3. For the colours are many, but the light is one.
4. Therefore thou writest that which is of mother of
   emerald, and of lapis-lazuli, and of turquoise, and of
   alexandrite.

5. Another writeth the words of topaz, and of deep amethyst, and of gray sapphire, and of deep sapphire with a tinge as of blood.

6. Therefore do ye fret yourselves because of this.

7. Be not contented with the image.

8. I who am the Image of an Image say this.

9. Debate not of the image, saying Beyond! Beyond!

   One mounteth unto the Crown by the moon and by the Sun, and by the arrow, and by the Foundation, and by the dark home of the stars from the black earth.

10. Not otherwise may ye reach unto the Smooth Point.

11. Nor is it fitting for the cobbler to prate of the Royal matter. O cobbler! mend me this shoe, that I may walk. O king! if I be thy son, let us speak of the Embassy to the King thy Brother.

12. Then was there silence. Speech had done with us awhile.

   There is a light so strenuous that it is not perceived as light.

13. Wolf's bane is not so sharp as steel; yet it pierceth the body more subtly.

14. Even as evil kisses corrupt the blood, so do my words devour the spirit of man.

15. I breathe, and there is infinite dis-ease in the spirit.

16. As an acid eats into steel, as a cancer that utterly corrupts the body; so am I unto the spirit of man.

17. I shall not rest until I have dissolved it all.

18. So also the light that is absorbed. One absorbs little, and is called white and glistening; one absorbs all and is called black.

19. Therefore, O my darling, art thou black.

20. O my beautiful, I have likened thee to a jet Nubian slave, a boy of melancholy eyes.

21. O the filthy one! the dog! they cry against thee.
    Because thou art my beloved.
22. Happy are they that praise thee; for they see thee with Mine eyes.
23. Not aloud shall they praise thee; but in the night watch one shall steal close, and grip thee with the secret grip; another shall privily cast a crown of violets over thee; a third shall greatly dare, and press mad lips to thine.
24. Yea! the night shall cover all, the night shall cover all.
25. Thou wast long seeking Me; thou didst run forward so fast that I was unable to come up with thee.
    O thou darling fool! what bitterness thou didst crown thy days withal.
26. Now I am with thee; I will never leave thy being.
27. For I am the soft sinuous one entwined about thee, heart of gold!
28. My head is jewelled with twelve stars; My body is white as milk of the stars; it is bright with the blue of the abyss of stars invisible.
29. I have found that which could not be found; I have found a vessel of quicksilver.
30. Thou shalt instruct thy servant in his ways, thou shalt speak often with him.
31. (The scribe looketh upwards and crieth) Amen! Thou hast spoken it, Lord God!
32. Further Adonai spake unto V.V.V.V.V. and said:
33. Let us take our delight in the multitude of men!
    Let us shape unto ourselves a boat of mother-of-pearl from them, that we may ride upon the river of Amrit!
34. Thou seest yon petal of amaranth, blown by the wind from the low sweet brows of Hathor?
35. (The Magister saw it and rejoiced in the beauty of it.) Listen!

36. (From a certain world came an infinite wail.)

    That falling petal seemed to the little ones a wave to engulph their continent.

37. So they will reproach thy servant, saying: Who hath set thee to save us?

38. He will be sore distressed.

39. All they understand not that thou and I are fashioning a boat of mother-of-pearl. We will sail down the river of Amrit even to the yew-groves of Yama, where we may rejoice exceedingly.

40. The joy of men shall be our silver gleam, their woe our blue gleam—all in the mother-of-pearl.

41. (The scribe was wroth thereat. He spake:

    O Adonai and my master, I have borne the inkhorn and the pen without pay, in order that I might search this river of Amrit, and sail thereon as one of ye. This I demand for my fee, that I partake of the echo of your kisses.)

42. (And immediately it was granted unto him.)

43. (Nay; but not therewith was he content. By an infinite abasement unto shame did he strive. Then a voice:)

44. Thou strivest ever; even in thy yielding thou strivest to yield—and lo! thou yieldest not.

45. Go thou unto the outermost places and subdue all things.

46. Subdue thy fear and thy disgust. Then—yield!

47. There was a maiden that strayed among the corn, and sighed; then grew a new birth, a narcissus, and therein she forgot her sighing and her loneliness.

48. Even instantly rode Hades heavily upon her, and ravished her away.

49. (Then the scribe knew the narcissus in his heart; but because it came not to his lips, therefore was he shamed and spake no more.)

50. Adonai spake yet again with V.V.V.V.V. and said:
     The earth is ripe for vintage; let us eat of her grapes, and be drunken thereon.
51. And V.V.V.V.V. answered and said: O my lord, my dove, my excellent one, how shall this word seem unto the children of men?
52. And He answered him: Not as thou canst see.
     It is certain that every letter of this cipher hath some value; but who shall determine the value? For it varieth ever, according to the subtlety of Him that made it.
53. And He answered Him: Have I not the key thereof?
     I am clothed with the body of flesh; I am one with the Eternal and Omnipotent God.
54. Then said Adonai: Thou hast the Head of the Hawk, and thy Phallus is the Phallus of Asar. Thou knowest the white, and thou knowest the black, and thou knowest that these are one. But why seekest thou the knowledge of their equivalence?
55. And he said: That my Work may be right.
56. And Adonai said: The strong brown reaper swept his swathe and rejoiced. The wise man counted his muscles, and pondered, and understood not, and was sad.
     Reap thou, and rejoice!
57. Then was the Adept glad, and lifted his arm.
     Lo! an earthquake, and plague, and terror on the earth!
     A casting down of them that sate in high places; a famine upon the multitude!
58. And the grape fell ripe and rich into his mouth.
59. Stained is the purple of thy mouth, O brilliant one, with the white glory of the lips of Adonai.
60. The foam of the grape is like the storm upon the sea; the ships tremble and shudder; the shipmaster is afraid.

61. That is thy drunkenness, O holy one, and the winds whirl away the soul of the scribe into the happy haven.

62. O Lord God! let the haven be cast down by the fury of the storm! Let the foam of the grape tincture my soul with Thy light!

63. Bacchus grew old, and was Silenus; Pan was ever Pan for ever and ever more throughout the æons.

64. Intoxicate the inmost, O my lover, not the outermost!

65. So was it—ever the same! I have aimed at the peeled wand of my God, and I have hit; yea, I have hit.

# II

1. I passed into the mountain of lapis-lazuli, even as a green hawk between the pillars of turquoise that is seated upon the throne of the East.
2. So came I to Duant, the starry abode, and I heard voices crying aloud.
3. O Thou that sittest upon the Earth! (so spake a certain Veiled One to me) thou art not greater than thy mother! Thou speck of dust infinitesimal!
    Thou art the Lord of Glory, and the unclean dog.
4. Stooping down, dipping my wings, I came unto the darkly-splendid abodes. There in that formless abyss was I made a partaker of the Mysteries Averse.
5. I suffered the deadly embrace of the Snake and of the Goat; I paid the infernal homage to the shame of Khem.
6. Therein was this virtue, that the One became the all.
7. Moreover I beheld a vision of a river. There was a little boat thereon; and in it under purple sails was a golden woman, an image of Asi wrought in finest gold. Also the river was of blood, and the boat of shining steel. Then I loved her; and, loosing my girdle, cast myself into the stream.
8. I gathered myself into the little boat, and for many days and nights did I love her, burning beautiful incense before her.
9. Yea! I gave her of the flower of my youth.
10. But she stirred not; only by my kisses I defiled her so that she turned to blackness before me.

11. Yet I worshipped her, and gave her of the flower of my youth.

12. Also it came to pass, that thereby she sickened, and corrupted before me. Almost I cast myself into the stream.

13. Then at the end appointed her body was whiter than the milk of the stars, and her lips red and warm as the sunset, and her life of a white heat like the heat of the midmost sun.

14. Then rose she up from the abyss of Ages of Sleep, and her body embraced me. Altogether I melted into her beauty and was glad.

15. The river also became the river of Amrit, and the little boat was the chariot of the flesh, and the sails thereof the blood of the heart that beareth me, that beareth me.

16. O serpent woman of the stars! I, even I, have fashioned Thee from a pale image of fine gold.

17. Also the Holy One came upon me, and I beheld a white swan floating in the blue.

18. Between its wings I sate, and the æons fled away.

19. Then the swan flew and dived and soared, yet no whither we went.

20. A little crazy boy that rode with me spake unto the swan, and said:

21. Who art thou that dost float and fly and dive and soar in the inane? Behold, these many æons have passed; whence camest thou? Whither wilt thou go?

22. And laughing I chid him, saying: No whence! No whither!

23. The swan being silent, he answered: Then, if with no goal, why this eternal journey?

24. And I laid my head against the Head of the Swan, and laughed, saying: Is there not joy ineffable in this aimless

winging? Is there not weariness and impatience for who would attain to some goal?

25. And the swan was ever silent. Ah! but we floated in the infinite Abyss. Joy! Joy!

   White swan, bear thou ever me up between thy wings!

26. O silence! O rapture! O end of things visible and invisible! This is all mine, who am Not.

27. Radiant God! Let me fashion an image of gems and gold for Thee! that the people may cast it down and trample it to dust! That Thy glory may be seen of them.

28. Nor shall it be spoken in the markets that I am come who should come; but Thy coming shall be the one word.

29. Thou shalt manifest Thyself in the unmanifest; in the secret places men shall meet with thee, and Thou shalt overcome them.

30. I saw a pale sad boy that lay upon the marble in the sunlight, and wept. By his side was the forgotten lute. Ah! but he wept.

31. Then came an eagle from the abyss of glory and overshadowed him. So black was the shadow that he was no more visible.

32. But I heard the lute lively discoursing through the blue still air.

33. Ah! messenger of the beloved One, let Thy shadow be over me!

34. Thy name is Death, it may be, or Shame, or Love.

   So thou bringest me tidings of the Beloved One, I shall not ask thy name.

35. Where is now the Master? cry the little crazy boys.

He is dead! He is shamed! He is wedded! and their mockery shall ring round the world.

36. But the Master shall have had his reward.

The laughter of the mockers shall be a ripple in the hair of the Beloved One.

37. Behold! the Abyss of the Great Deep. Therein is a mighty dolphin, lashing his sides with the force of the waves.

38. There is also an harper of gold, playing infinite tunes.

39. Then the dolphin delighted therein, and put off his body, and became a bird.

40. The harper also laid aside his harp, and played infinite tunes upon the Pan-pipe.

41. Then the bird desired exceedingly this bliss, and laying down its wings became a faun of the forest.

42. The harper also laid down his Pan-pipe, and with the human voice sang his infinite tunes.

43. Then the faun was enraptured, and followed far; at last the harper was silent, and the faun became Pan in the midst of the primal forest of Eternity.

44. Thou canst not charm the dolphin with silence, O my prophet!

45. Then the adept was rapt away in bliss, and the beyond of bliss, and exceeded the excess of excess.

46. Also his body shook and staggered with the burden of that bliss and that excess and that ultimate nameless.

47. They cried He is drunk or He is mad or He is in pain or He is about to die; and he heard them not.

48. O my Lord, my beloved! How shall I indite songs, when even the memory of the shadow of thy glory is a thing beyond all music of speech or of silence?

49. Behold! I am a man. Even a little child might not endure Thee. And lo!

50. I was alone in a great park, and by a certain hillock was a ring of deep enamelled grass wherein green-clad ones, most beautiful, played.

51. In their play I came even unto the land of Fairy Sleep.
     All my thoughts were clad in green; most beautiful were they.

52. All night they danced and sang; but Thou art the morning, O my darling, my serpent that twinest Thee about this heart.

53. I am the heart, and Thou the serpent. Wind Thy coils closer about me, so that no light nor bliss may penetrate.

54. Crush out the blood of me, as a grape upon the tongue of a white Doric girl that languishes with her lover in the moonlight.

55. Then let the End awake. Long hast thou slept, O great God Terminus! Long ages hast thou waited at the end of the city and the roads thereof.
     Awake Thou! wait no more!

56. Nay, Lord! but I am come to Thee. It is I that wait at last.

57. The prophet cried against the mountain; come thou hither, that I may speak with thee!

58. The mountain stirred not. Therefore went the prophet unto the mountain, and spake unto it. But the feet of the prophet were weary, and the mountain heard not his voice.

59. But I have called unto Thee, and I have journeyed unto Thee, and it availed me not.

60. I waited patiently, and Thou wast with me from the beginning.

61. This now I know, O my beloved, and we are stretched at our ease among the vines.

62. But these thy prophets; they must cry aloud and scourge

themselves; they must cross trackless wastes and un-fathomed oceans; to await Thee is the end, not the beginning.

63. Let darkness cover up the writing! Let the scribe depart among his ways.

64. But thou and I are stretched at our ease among the vines; what is he?

65. O Thou beloved One! is there not an end? Nay, but there is an end. Awake! arise! gird up thy limbs, O thou runner; bear thou the Word unto the mighty cities, yea, unto the mighty cities.

# III

1. Verily and Amen! I passed through the deep sea, and by the rivers of running water that abound therein, and I came unto the Land of No Desire.
2. Wherein was a white unicorn with a silver collar, whereon was graven the aphorism Linea viridis gyrat universa.
3. Then the word of Adonai came unto me by the mouth of the Magister mine, saying: O heart that art girt about with the coils of the old serpent, lift up thyself unto the mountain of initiation!
4. But I remembered. Yea, Than, yea, Theli, yea, Lilith! these three were about me from of old. For they are one.
5. Beautiful wast thou, O Lilith, thou serpent-woman!
6. Thou wast lithe and delicious to the taste, and thy perfume was of musk mingled with ambergris.
7. Close didst thou cling with thy coils unto the heart, and it was as the joy of all the spring.
8. But I beheld in thee a certain taint, even in that wherein I delighted.
9. I beheld in thee the taint of thy father the ape, of thy grandsire the Blind Worm of Slime.
10. I gazed upon the Crystal of the Future, and I saw the horror of the End of thee.
11. Further, I destroyed the time Past, and the time to Come—had I not the Power of the Sand-glass?
12. But in the very hour I beheld corruption.

13. Then I said: O my beloved, O Lord Adonai, I pray thee to loosen the coils of the serpent!

14. But she was closed fast upon me, so that my Force was stayed in its inception.

15. Also I prayed unto the Elephant God, the Lord of Beginnings, who breaketh down obstruction.

16. These gods came right quickly to mine aid. I beheld them; I joined myself unto them; I was lost in their vastness.

17. Then I beheld myself compassed about with the Infinite Circle of Emerald that encloseth the Universe.

18. O Snake of Emerald, Thou hast no time Past, no time To Come. Verily Thou art not.

19. Thou art delicious beyond all taste and touch, Thou art not-to-be-beheld for glory, Thy voice is beyond the Speech and the Silence and the Speech therein, and Thy perfume is of pure ambergris, that is not weighed against the finest gold of the fine gold.

20. Also Thy coils are of infinite range; the Heart that Thou dost encircle is an Universal Heart.

21. I, and Me, and Mine were sitting with lutes in the market-place of the great city, the city of the violets and the roses.

22. The night fell, and the music of the lutes was stilled.

23. The tempest arose, and the music of the lutes was stilled.

24. The hour passed, and the music of the lutes was stilled.

25. But Thou art Eternity and Space; Thou art Matter and Motion; and Thou art the negation of all these things.

26. For there is no Symbol of Thee.

27. If I say Come up upon the mountains! the celestial waters flow at my word. But thou art the Water beyond the waters.

28. The red three-angled heart hath been set up in Thy

shrine; for the priests despised equally the shrine and the god.

29. Yet all the while Thou wast hidden therein, as the Lord of Silence is hidden in the buds of the lotus.

30. Thou art Sebek the crocodile against Asar; thou art Mati, the Slayer in the Deep. Thou art Typhon, the Wrath of the Elements, O Thou who transcendest the Forces in their Concourse and Cohesion, in their Death and their Disruption. Thou art Python, the terrible serpent about the end of all things!

31. I turned me about thrice in every way; and always I came at the last unto Thee.

32. Many things I beheld mediate and immediate; but, beholding them no more, I beheld Thee.

33. Come thou, O beloved One, O Lord God of the Universe, O Vast One, O Minute One! I am Thy beloved.

34. All day I sing of Thy delight; all night I delight in Thy song.

35. There is no other day or night than this.

36. Thou art beyond the day and the night; I am Thyself, O my Maker, my Master, my Mate!

37. I am like the little red dog that sitteth upon the knees of the Unknown.

38. Thou hast brought me into great delight. Thou hast given me of Thy flesh to eat and of Thy blood for an offering of intoxication.

39. Thou hast fastened the fangs of Eternity in my soul, and the Poison of the Infinite hath consumed me utterly.

40. I am become like a luscious devil of Italy; a fair strong woman with worn cheeks, eaten out with hunger for kisses. She hath played the harlot in divers palaces; she hath given her body to the beasts.

41. She hath slain her kinsfolk with strong venom of toads;
    she hath been scourged with many rods.
42. She hath been broken in pieces upon the Wheel; the
    hands of the hangman have bound her unto it.
43. The fountains of water have been loosed upon her; she
    hath struggled with exceeding torment.
44. She hath burst in sunder with the weight of the waters;
    she hath sunk into the awful Sea.
45. So am I, O Adonai, my lord, and such are the waters of
    Thine intolerable Essence.
46. So am I, O Adonai, my beloved, and Thou hast burst
    me utterly in sunder.
47. I am shed out like spilt blood upon the mountains; the
    Ravens of Dispersion have borne me utterly away.
48. Therefore is the seal unloosed, that guarded the Eighth
    abyss; therefore is the vast sea as a veil; therefore is there
    a rending asunder of all things.
49. Yea, also verily Thou art the cool still water of the
    wizard fount. I have bathed in Thee, and lost me in
    Thy stillness.
50. That which went in as a brave boy of beautiful limbs
    cometh forth as a maiden, as a little child for perfection.
51. O Thou light and delight, ravish me away into the
    milky ocean of the stars!
52. O Thou Son of a light-transcending mother, blessed be
    Thy name, and the Name of Thy Name, throughout the
    ages!
53. Behold! I am a butterfly at the Source of Creation; let
    me die before the hour, falling dead into Thine infinite
    stream!
54. Also the stream of the stars floweth ever majestical unto
    the Abode; bear me away upon the Bosom of Nuit!
55. This is the world of the waters of Maim; this is the

bitter water that becometh sweet. Thou art beautiful and bitter, O golden one, O my Lord Adonai, O thou Abyss of Sapphire!

56. I follow Thee, and the waters of Death fight strenuously against me. I pass unto the Waters beyond Death and beyond Life.

57. How shall I answer the foolish man? In no way shall he come to the Identity of Thee!

58. But I am the Fool that heedeth not the Play of the Magician. Me doth the Woman of the Mysteries instruct in vain; I have burst the bonds of Love and of Power and of Worship.

59. Therefore is the Eagle made one with the Man, and the gallows of infamy dance with the fruit of the just.

60. I have descended, O my darling, into the black shining waters, and I have plucked Thee forth as a black pearl of infinite preciousness.

61. I have gone down, O my God, into the abyss of the all, and I have found Thee in the midst under the guise of No Thing.

62. But as Thou art the Last, Thou art also the Next, and as the Next do I reveal Thee to the multitude.

63. They that ever desired Thee shall obtain Thee, even at the End of their Desire.

64. Glorious, glorious, glorious art Thou, O my lover supernal, O Self of myself.

65. For I have found Thee alike in the Me and the Thee; there is no difference, O my beautiful, my desirable One! In the One and the Many have I found Thee; yea, I have found Thee.

# IV

1. O crystal heart! I the Serpent clasp Thee; I drive home mine head into the central core of Thee, O God my beloved.

2. Even as on the resounding wind-swept heights of Mitylene some god-like woman casts aside the lyre, and with her locks aflame as an aureole, plunges into the wet heart of the creation, so I, O Lord my God!

3. There is a beauty unspeakable in this heart of corruption, where the flowers are aflame.

4. Ah me! but the thirst of Thy joy parches up this throat, so that I cannot sing.

5. I will make me a little boat of my tongue, and explore the unknown rivers. It may be that the everlasting salt may turn to sweetness, and that my life may be no longer athirst.

6. O ye that drink of the brine of your desire, ye are nigh to madness! Your torture increaseth as ye drink, yet still ye drink. Come up through the creeks to the fresh water; I shall be waiting for you with my kisses.

7. As the bezoar-stone that is found in the belly of the cow, so is my lover among lovers.

8. O honey boy! Bring me Thy cool limbs hither! Let us sit awhile in the orchard, until the sun go down! Let us feast on the cool grass! Bring wine, ye slaves, that the cheeks of my boy may flush red.

9. In the garden of immortal kisses, O thou brilliant One,

shine forth! Make Thy mouth an opium-poppy, that one kiss is the key to the infinite sleep and lucid, the sleep of Shi-loh-am.

10. In my sleep I beheld the Universe like a clear crystal without one speck.

11. There are purse-proud penniless ones that stand at the door of the tavern and prate of their feats of wine-bibbing.

12. There are purse-proud penniless ones that stand at the door of the tavern and revile the guests.

13. The guests dally upon couches of mother-of-pearl in the garden; the noise of the foolish men is hidden from them.

14. Only the inn-keeper feareth lest the favour of the king be withdrawn from him.

15. Thus spake the Magister V.V.V.V.V. unto Adonai his God, as they played together in the starlight over against the deep black pool that is in the Holy Place of the Holy House beneath the Altar of the Holiest One.

16. But Adonai laughed, and played more languidly.

17. Then the scribe took note, and was glad. But Adonai had no fear of the Magician and his play.

    For it was Adonai who had taught all his tricks to the Magician.

18. And the Magister entered into the play of the Magician. When the Magician laughed he laughed; all as a man should do.

19. And Adonai said: Thou art enmeshed in the web of the Magician. This He said subtly, to try him.

20. But the Magister gave the sign of the Magistry, and laughed back on Him: O Lord, O beloved, did these fingers relax on Thy curls, or these eyes turn away from Thine eye?

21. And Adonai delighted in him exceedingly.

22. Yea, O my master, thou art the beloved of the Beloved One; the Bennu Bird is set up in Philæ not in vain.

23. I who was the priestess of Ahathoor rejoice in your love. Arise, O Nile-God, and devour the holy place of the Cow of Heaven! Let the milk of the stars be drunk up by Sebek the dweller of Nile!

24. Arise, O serpent Apep, Thou art Adonai the beloved one! Thou art my darling and my lord, and Thy poison is sweeter than the kisses of Isis the mother of the Gods!

25. For Thou art He! Yea, Thou shalt swallow up Asi and Asar, and the children of Ptah. Thou shalt pour forth a flood of poison to destroy the works of the Magician. Only the Destroyer shall devour Thee; Thou shalt blacken his throat, wherein his spirit abideth. Ah, serpent Apep, but I love Thee!

26. My God! Let Thy secret fang pierce to the marrow of the little secret bone that I have kept against the Day of Vengeance of Hoor-Ra. Let Kheph-Ra sound his sharded drone! let the jackals of Day and Night howl in the wilderness of Time! let the Towers of the Universe totter, and the guardians hasten away! For my Lord hath revealed Himself as a mighty serpent, and my heart is the blood of His body.

27. I am like a love-sick courtesan of Corinth. I have toyed with kings and captains, and made them my slaves. To-day I am the slave of the little asp of death; and who shall loosen our love?

28. Weary, weary! saith the scribe, who shall lead me to the sight of the Rapture of my master?

29. The body is weary and the soul is sore weary and sleep weighs down their eyelids; yet ever abides the sure consciousness of ecstacy, unknown, yet known in that its being

is certain. O Lord, be my helper, and bring me to the bliss of the Beloved!

30. I came to the house of the Beloved, and the wine was like fire that flieth with green wings through the world of waters.

31. I felt the red lips of nature and the black lips of perfection. Like sisters they fondled me their little brother; they decked me out as a bride; they mounted me for Thy bridal chamber.

32. They fled away at Thy coming; I was alone before Thee.

33. I trembled at Thy coming, O my God, for Thy messenger was more terrible than the Death-star.

34. On the threshold stood the fulminant figure of Evil, the Horror of emptiness, with his ghastly eyes like poisonous wells. He stood, and the chamber was corrupt; the air stank. He was an old and gnarled fish more hideous than the shells of Abaddon.

35. He enveloped me with his demon tentacles; yea, the eight fears took hold upon me.

36. But I was anointed with the right sweet oil of the Magister; I slipped from the embrace as a stone from the sling of a boy of the woodlands.

37. I was smooth and hard as ivory; the horror gat no hold. Then at the noise of the wind of Thy coming he was dissolved away, and the abyss of the great void was unfolded before me.

38. Across the waveless sea of eternity Thou didst ride with Thy captains and Thy hosts; with Thy chariots and horsemen and spearmen didst Thou travel through the blue.

39. Before I saw Thee Thou wast already with me; I was smitten through by Thy marvellous spear.

40. I was stricken as a bird by the bolt of the thunderer; I was pierced as the thief by the Lord of the Garden.

41. O my Lord, let us sail upon the sea of blood!

42. There is a deep taint beneath the ineffable bliss; it is the taint of generation.

43. Yea, though the flower wave bright in the sunshine, the root is deep in the darkness of earth.

44. Praise to thee, O beautiful dark earth, thou art the mother of a million myriads of myriads of flowers.

45. Also I beheld my God, and the countenance of Him was a thousandfold brighter than the lightning. Yet in his heart I beheld the slow and dark One, the ancient one, the devourer of His children.

46. In the height and the abyss, O my beautiful, there is no thing, verily, there is no thing at all, that is not altogether and perfectly fashioned for Thy delight.

47. Light cleaveth unto Light, and filth to filth; with pride one contemneth another. But not Thou, who art all, and beyond it; who art absolved from the Division of the Shadows.

48. O day of Eternity, let Thy wave break in foamless glory of sapphire upon the laborious coral of our making!

49. We have made us a ring of glistening white sand, strewn wisely in the midst of the Delightful Ocean.

50. Let the palms of brilliance flower upon our island; we shall eat of their fruit, and be glad.

51. But for me the lustral water, the great ablution, the dissolving of the soul in that resounding abyss.

52. I have a little son like a wanton goat; my daughter is like an unfledged eaglet; they shall get them fins, that they may swim.

53. That they may swim, O my beloved, swim far in the warm honey of Thy being, O blessed one, O boy of beatitude!

54. This heart of mine is girt about with the serpent that devoureth his own coils.

55. When shall there be an end, O my darling, O when shall the Universe and the Lord thereof be utterly swallowed up?

56. Nay! who shall devour the Infinite? who shall undo the Wrong of the Beginning?

57. Thou criest like a white cat upon the roof of the Universe; there is none to answer Thee.

58. Thou art like a lonely pillar in the midst of the sea; there is none to behold Thee, O Thou who beholdest all!

59. Thou dost faint, thou dost fail, thou scribe; cried the desolate Voice; but I have filled thee with a wine whose savour thou knowest not.

60. It shall avail to make drunken the people of the old gray sphere that rolls in the infinite Far-off; they shall lap the wine as dogs that lap the blood of a beautiful courtesan pierced through by the Spear of a swift rider through the city.

61. I too am the Soul of the desert; thou shalt seek me yet again in the wilderness of sand.

62. At thy right hand a great lord and a comely; at thy left hand a woman clad in gossamer and gold and having the stars in her hair. Ye shall journey far into a land of pestilence and evil; ye shall encamp in the river of a foolish city forgotten; there shall ye meet with Me.

63. There will I make Mine habitation; as for bridal will I come bedecked and anointed; there shall the Consummation be accomplished.

64. O my darling, I also wait for the brilliance of the hour ineffable, when the universe shall be like a girdle for the midst of the ray of our love, extending beyond the permitted end of the endless One.

65. Then, O thou heart, will I the serpent eat thee wholly up; yea, I will eat thee wholly up.

# V

1. Ah! my Lord Adonai, that dalliest with the Magister in the Treasure-House of Pearls, let me listen to the echo of your kisses.
2. Is not the starry heaven shaken as a leaf at the tremulous rapture of your love? Am not I the flying spark of light whirled away by the great wind of your perfection?
3. Yea, cried the Holy One, and from Thy spark will I the Lord kindle a great light; I will burn through the grey city in the old and desolate land; I will cleanse it from its great impurity.
4. And thou, O prophet, shalt see these things, and thou shalt heed them not.
5. Now is the Pillar established in the Void; now is Asi fulfilled of Asar; now is Hoor let down into the Animal Soul of Things like a fiery star that falleth upon the darkness of the earth.
6. Through the midnight thou art dropt, O my child, my conqueror, my sword-girt captain, O Hoor! and they shall find thee as a black gnarl'd glittering stone, and they shall worship thee.
7. My prophet shall prophesy concerning thee; around thee the maidens shall dance, and bright babes be born unto them. Thou shalt inspire the proud ones with infinite pride, and the humble ones with an ecstasy of abasement; all this shall transcend the Known and the Unknown with somewhat that hath no name. For it is as the abyss of the Arcanum that is opened in the secret Place of Silence.

8. Thou hast come hither, O my prophet, through grave paths. Thou hast eaten of the dung of the Abominable Ones; thou hast prostrated thyself before the Goat and the Crocodile; the evil men have made thee a plaything; thou hast wandered as a painted harlot, ravishing with sweet scent and Chinese colouring, in the streets; thou hast darkened thine eyepits with Kohl; thou hast tinted thy lips with vermilion; thou hast plastered thy cheeks with ivory enamels. Thou hast played the wanton in every gate and by-way of the great city. The men of the city have lusted after thee to abuse thee and to beat thee. They have mouthed the golden spangles of fine dust wherewith thou didst bedeck thine hair; they have scourged the painted flesh of thee with their whips; thou hast suffered unspeakable things.

9. But I have burnt within thee as a pure flame without oil. In the midnight I was brighter than the moon; in the daytime I exceeded utterly the sun; in the byways of thy being I flamed, and dispelled the illusion.

10. Therefore thou art wholly pure before Me; therefore thou art My virgin unto eternity.

11. Therefore I love thee with surpassing love; therefore they that despise thee shall adore thee.

12. Thou shalt be lovely and pitiful toward them; thou shalt heal them of the unutterable evil.

13. They shall change in their destruction, even as two dark stars that crash together in the abyss, and blaze up in an infinite burning.

14. All this while did Adonai pierce my being with his sword that hath four blades; the blade of the thunderbolt, the blade of the Pylon, the blade of the serpent, the blade of the Phallus.

15. Also he taught me the holy unutterable word Ararita, so that I melted the sixfold gold into a single invisible point, whereof naught may be spoken.

16. For the Magistry of this Opus is a secret magistry and the sign of the master thereof is a certain ring of lapis-lazuli with the name of my master, who am I, and the Eye in the Midst thereof.

17. Also He spake and said: This is a secret sign, and thou shalt not disclose it unto the profane, nor unto the neophyte, nor unto the zelator, nor unto the practicus, nor unto the philosophus, nor unto the lesser adept, nor unto the greater adept.

18. But unto the exempt adept thou shalt disclose thyself if thou have need of him for the lesser operations of thine art.

19. Accept the worship of the foolish people, whom thou hatest. The Fire is not defiled by the altars of the Ghebers, nor is the Moon contaminated by the incense of them that adore the Queen of Night.

20. Thou shalt dwell among the people as a precious diamond among cloudy diamonds, and crystals, and pieces of glass. Only the eye of the just merchant shall behold thee, and plunging in his hand shall single thee out and glorify thee before men.

21. But thou shalt heed none of this. Thou shalt be ever the heart, and I the serpent will coil close about thee. My coils shall never relax throughout the æons. Neither change nor sorrow nor unsubstantiality shall have thee; for thou art passed beyond all these.

22. Even as the diamond shall glow red for the rose, and green for the rose-leaf; so shalt thou abide apart from the Impressions.

23. I am thou, and the Pillar is 'stablished in the void.

24. Also thou art beyond the stabilities of Being and of Consciousness and of Bliss; for I am thou, and the Pillar is 'stablished in the void.

25. Also thou shalt discourse of these things unto the man

that writeth them, and he shall partake of them as a sacrament; for I who am thou am he, and the Pillar is 'stablished in the void.

26. From the Crown to the Abyss, so goeth it single and erect. Also the limitless sphere shall glow with the brilliance thereof.

27. Thou shalt rejoice in the pools of adorable water; thou shalt bedeck thy damsels with pearls of fecundity; thou shalt light flame like licking tongues of liquor of the Gods between the pools.

28. Also thou shalt convert the all-sweeping air into the winds of pale water, thou shalt transmute the earth into a blue abyss of wine.

29. Ruddy are the gleams of ruby and gold that sparkle therein; one drop shall intoxicate the Lord of the Gods my servant.

30. Also Adonai spake unto V.V.V.V.V. saying: O my little one, my tender one, my little amorous one, my gazelle, my beautiful, my boy, let us fill up the pillar of the Infinite with an infinite kiss!

31. So that the stable was shaken and the unstable became still.

32. They that beheld it cried with a formidable affright: The end of things is come upon us.

33. And it was even so.

34. Also I was in the spirit vision and beheld a parricidal pomp of atheists, coupled by two and by two in the supernal ecstasy of the stars. They did laugh and rejoice exceedingly, being clad in purple robes and drunken with purple wine, and their whole soul was one purple flower-flame of holiness.

35. They beheld not God; they beheld not the Image of God; therefore were they arisen to the Palace of the Splendour Ineffable. A sharp sword smote out before

them, and the worm Hope writhed in its death-agony under their feet.

36. Even as their rapture shore asunder the visible Hope, so also the Fear Invisible fled away and was no more.

37. O ye that are beyond Aormuzdi and Ahrimanes! blessèd are ye unto the ages.

38. They shaped Doubt as a sickle, and reaped the flowers of Faith for their garlands.

39. They shaped Ecstasy as a spear, and pierced the ancient dragon that sat upon the stagnant water.

40. Then the fresh springs were unloosed, that the folk athirst might be at ease.

41. And again I was caught up into the presence of my Lord Adonai, and the knowledge and Conversation of the Holy One, the Angel that Guardeth me.

42. O Holy Exalted One, O Self beyond self, O Self-Luminous Image of the Unimaginable Naught, O my darling, my beautiful, come Thou forth and follow me.

43. Adonai, divine Adonai, let Adonai initiate refulgent dalliance! Thus I concealed the name of Her name that inspireth my rapture, the scent of whose body bewildereth the soul, the light of whose soul abaseth this body unto the beasts.

44. I have sucked out the blood with my lips; I have drained Her beauty of its sustenance; I have abased Her before me, I have mastered Her, I have possessed Her, and Her life is within me. In Her blood I inscribe the secret riddles of the Sphinx of the Gods, that none shall understand, — save only the pure and voluptuous, the chaste and obscene, the androgyne and the gynander that have passed beyond the bars of the prison that the old Slime of Khem set up in the Gates of Amennti.

45. O my adorable, my delicious one, all night will I pour

out the libation on Thine altars; all night will I burn the sacrifice of blood; all night will I swing the thurible of my delight before Thee, and the fervour of the orisons shall intoxicate Thy nostrils.

46. O Thou who camest from the land of the Elephant, girt about with the tiger's pell, and garlanded with the lotus of the spirit, do Thou inebriate my life with Thy madness, that She leap at my passing.

47. Bid Thy maidens who follow Thee bestrew us a bed of flowers immortal, that we may take our pleasure thereupon. Bid Thy satyrs heap thorns among the flowers, that we may take our pain thereupon. Let the pleasure and pain be mingled in one supreme offering unto the Lord Adonai!

48. Also I heard the voice of Adonai the Lord the desirable one concerning that which is beyond.

49. Let not the dwellers in Thebai and the temples thereof prate ever of the Pillars of Hercules and the Ocean of the West. Is not the Nile a beautiful water?

50. Let not the priest of Isis uncover the nakedness of Nuit, for every step is a death and a birth. The priest of Isis lifted the veil of Isis, and was slain by the kisses of her mouth. Then was he the priest of Nuit, and drank of the milk of the stars.

51. Let not the failure and the pain turn aside the worshippers. The foundations of the pyramid were hewn in the living rock ere sunset; did the king weep at dawn that the crown of the pyramid was yet unquarried in the distant land?

52. There was also an humming-bird that spake unto the horned cerastes, and prayed him for poison. And the great snake of Khem the Holy One, the royal Uræus serpent, answered him and said:

53. I sailed over the sky of Nu in the car called

Millions-of-Years, and I saw not any creature upon Seb
that was equal to me. The venom of my fang is the
inheritance of my father, and of my father's father; and
how shall I give it unto thee? Live thou and thy
children as I and my fathers have lived, even unto an
hundred millions of generations, and it may be that the
mercy of the Mighty Ones may bestow upon thy
children a drop of the poison of eld.

54. Then the humming-bird was afflicted in his spirit, and
he flew unto the flowers, and it was as if naught had
been spoken between them. Yet in a little while a
serpent struck him that he died.

55. But an Ibis that meditated upon the bank of Nile the
beautiful god listened and heard. And he laid aside his
Ibis ways, and became as a serpent, saying Peradventure
in an hundred millions of millions of generations of my
children, they shall attain to a drop of the poison of the
fang of the Exalted One.

56. And behold! ere the moon waxed thrice he became an
Uræus serpent, and the poison of the fang was
established in him and his seed even for ever and for
ever.

57. O thou Serpent Apep, my Lord Adonai, it is a speck of
minutest time, this travelling through eternity, and in
Thy sight the landmarks are of fair white marble
untouched by the tool of the graver. Therefore Thou
art mine, even now and for ever and for everlasting.
Amen.

58. Moreover, I heard the voice of Adonai: Seal up the
book of the Heart and the Serpent; in the number five
and sixty seal thou the holy book.

   As fine gold that is beaten into a diadem for the fair
queen of Pharaoh, as great stones that are cemented
together into the Pyramid of the ceremony of the Death

of Asar, so do thou bind together the words and the deeds, so that in all is one Thought of Me thy delight Adonai.

59. And I answered and said: It is done even according unto Thy word. And it was done. And they that read the book and debated thereon passed into the desolate land of Barren Words. And they that sealed up the book into their blood were the chosen of Adonai, and the Thought of Adonai was a Word and a Deed; and they abode in the Land that the far-off travellers call Naught.

60. O land beyond honey and spice and all perfection! I will dwell therein with my Lord for ever.

61. And the Lord Adonai delighteth in me, and I bear the Cup of His gladness unto the weary ones of the old grey land.

62. They that drink thereof are smitten of disease; the abomination hath hold upon them, and their torment is like the thick black smoke of the evil abode.

63. But the chosen ones drank thereof, and became even as my Lord, my beautiful, my desirable one. There is no wine like unto this wine.

64. They are gathered together into a glowing heart, as Ra that gathered his clouds about Him at eventide into a molten sea of joy; and the snake that is the crown of Ra bindeth them about with the golden girdle of the death-kisses.

65. So also is the end of the book, and the Lord Adonai is about it on all sides like a Thunderbolt, and a Pylon, and a Snake, and a Phallus, and in the midst thereof He is like the Woman that jetteth out the milk of the stars from her paps; yea, the milk of the stars from her paps.

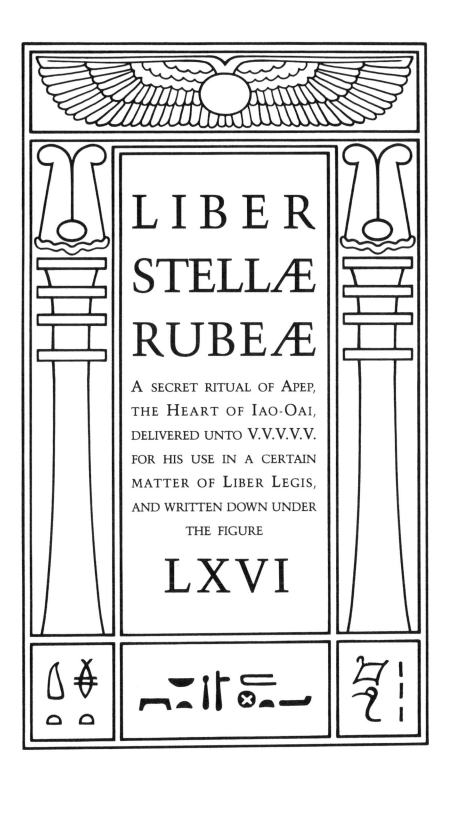

# LIBER STELLÆ RUBEÆ

A SECRET RITUAL OF APEP,
THE HEART OF IAO-OAI,
DELIVERED UNTO V.V.V.V.V.
FOR HIS USE IN A CERTAIN
MATTER OF LIBER LEGIS,
AND WRITTEN DOWN UNDER
THE FIGURE

# LXVI

A∴A∴
Publication in Class A.

1. Apep deifieth Asar.
2. Let excellent virgins evoke rejoicing, son of Night!
3. This is the book of the most secret cult of the Ruby Star. It shall be given to none, save to the shameless in deed as in word.
4. No man shall understand this writing—it is too subtle for the sons of men.
5. If the Ruby Star have shed its blood upon thee; if in the season of the moon thou hast invoked by the Iod and the Pe, then mayest thou partake of this most secret sacrament.
6. One shall instruct another, with no care for the matters of men's thought.
7. There shall be a fair altar in the midst, extended upon a black stone.
8. At the head of the altar gold, and twin images in green of the Master.
9. In the midst a cup of green wine.
10. At the foot the Star of Ruby.
11. The altar shall be entirely bare.
12. First, the ritual of the Flaming Star.
13. Next, the ritual of the Seal.
14. Next, the infernal adorations of OAI.

> Mu pa telai,
> Tu wa melai
> ā, ā, ā.
> Tu fu tulu!
> Tu fu tulu
> Pa, Sa, Ga.

Qwi Mu telai
Ya Pu melai;
ū, ū, ū.
'Se gu malai;
Pe fu telai,
Fu tu lu.

O chi balae
Wa pa malae:—
Ūt! Ūt! Ūt!
Ge; fu latrai,
Le fu malai
Kūt! Hūt! Nūt!

Al ŌĀĪ
Rel moai
Ti—Ti—Ti!
Wa la pelai
Tu fu latai
Wi, Ni, Bi.

15. Also thou shalt excite the wheels with the five wounds and the five wounds.
16. Then thou shalt excite the wheels with the two and the third in the midst; even ♄ and ♃, ☉ and ☽, ♂ and ♀, and ☿.
17. Then the five—and the sixth.
18. Also the altar shall fume before the master with incense that hath no smoke.
19. That which is to be denied shall be denied; that which is to be trampled shall be trampled; that which is to be spat upon shall be spat upon.
20. These things shall be burnt in the outer fire.
21. Then again the master shall speak as he will soft words, and with music and what else he will bring forward the Victim.

22. Also he shall slay a young child upon the altar, and the blood shall cover the altar with perfume as of roses.

23. Then shall the master appear as He should appear—in His glory.

24. He shall stretch himself upon the altar, and awake it into life, and into death.

25. (For so we conceal that life which is beyond.)

26. The temple shall be darkened, save for the fire and the lamp of the altar.

27. There shall he kindle a great fire and a devouring.

28. Also he shall smite the altar with his scourge, and blood shall flow therefrom.

29. Also he shall have made roses bloom thereon.

30. In the end he shall offer up the Vast Sacrifice, at the moment when the God licks up the flame upon the altar.

31. All these things shalt thou perform strictly, observing the time.

32. And the Beloved shall abide with Thee.

33. Thou shalt not disclose the interior world of this rite unto any one: therefore have I written it in symbols that cannot be understood.

34. I who reveal the ritual am IAO and OAI; the Right and the Averse.

35. These are alike unto me.

36. Now the Veil of this operation is called Shame, and the Glory abideth within.

37. Thou shalt comfort the heart of the secret stone with the warm blood. Thou shalt make a subtle decoction of delight, and the Watchers shall drink thereof.

38. I, Apep the Serpent, am the heart of IAO. Isis shall await Asar, and I in the midst.

39. Also the Priestess shall seek another altar, and perform my ceremonies thereon.

40. There shall be no hymn nor dithyramb in my praise and the praise of the rite, seeing that it is utterly beyond.
41. Thou shalt assure thyself of the stability of the altar.
42. In this rite thou shalt be alone.
43. I will give thee another ceremony whereby many shall rejoice.
44. Before all let the Oath be taken firmly as thou raisest up the altar from the black earth.
45. In the words that Thou knowest.
46. For I also swear unto thee by my body and soul that shall never be parted in sunder that I dwell within thee coiled and ready to spring.
47. I will give thee the kingdoms of the earth, O thou Who hast mastered the kingdoms of the East and of the West.
48. I am Apep, O thou slain One. Thou shalt slay thyself upon mine altar: I will have thy blood to drink.
49. For I am a mighty vampire, and my children shall suck up the wine of the earth which is blood.
50. Thou shalt replenish thy veins from the chalice of heaven.
51. Thou shalt be secret, a fear to the world.
52. Thou shalt be exalted, and none shall see thee; exalted, and none shall suspect thee.
53. For there are two glories diverse, and thou who hast won the first shalt enjoy the second.
54. I leap with joy within thee; my head is arisen to strike.
55. O the lust, the sheer rapture, of the life of the snake in the spine!
56. Mightier than God or man, I am in them, and pervade them.
57. Follow out these my words.
58. Fear nothing.
Fear nothing.
Fear nothing.

59. For I am nothing, and me thou shalt fear, O my virgin, my prophet within whose bowels I rejoice.

60. Thou shalt fear with the fear of love: I will overcome thee.

61. Thou shalt be very nigh to death.

62. But I will overcome thee; the New Life shall illumine thee with the Light that is beyond the Stars.

63. Thinkest thou? I, the force that have created all, am not to be despised.

64. And I will slay thee in my lust.

65. Thou shalt scream with the joy and the pain and the fear and the love—so that the ΛΟΓΟΣ of a new God leaps out among the Stars.

66. There shall be no sound heard but this thy lion-roar of rapture; yea, this thy lion-roar of rapture.

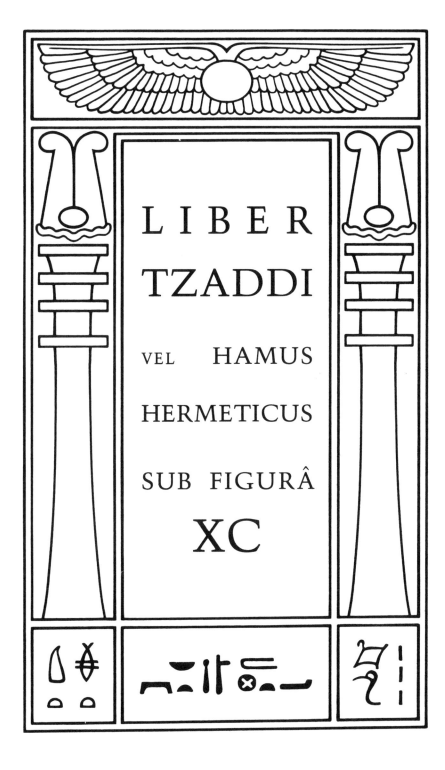

# LIBER TZADDI

## vel HAMUS HERMETICUS

### SUB FIGURÂ

## XC

A∴A∴
Publication in Class A.

0. In the name of the Lord of Initiation, Amen.
1. I fly and I alight as an hawk: of mother-of-emerald are my mighty-sweeping wings.
2. I swoop down upon the black earth; and it gladdens into green at my coming.
3. Children of Earth! rejoice! rejoice exceedingly; for your salvation is at hand.
4. The end of sorrow is come; I will ravish you away into mine unutterable joy.
5. I will kiss you, and bring you to the bridal: I will spread a feast before you in the house of happiness.
6. I am not come to rebuke you, or to enslave you.
7. I bid you not turn from your voluptuous ways, from your idleness, from your follies.
8. But I bring you joy to your pleasure, peace to your languor, wisdom to your folly.
9. All that ye do is right, if so be that ye enjoy it.
10. I am come against sorrow, against weariness, against them that seek to enslave you.
11. I pour you lustral wine, that giveth you delight both at the sunset and the dawn.
12. Come with me, and I will give you all that is desirable upon the earth.
13. Because I give you that of which Earth and its joys are but as shadows.
14. They flee away, but my joy abideth even unto the end.

15. I have hidden myself beneath a mask: I am a black and terrible God.

16. With courage conquering fear shall ye approach me: ye shall lay down your heads upon mine altar, expecting the sweep of the sword.

17. But the first kiss of love shall be radiant on your lips; and all my darkness and terror shall turn to light and joy.

18. Only those who fear shall fail. Those who have bent their backs to the yoke of slavery until they can no longer stand upright; them will I despise.

19. But you who have defied the law; you who have conquered by subtlety or force; you will I take unto me, even I will take you unto me.

20. I ask you to sacrifice nothing at mine altar; I am the God who giveth all.

21. Light, Life, Love; Force, Fantasy, Fire; these do I bring you: mine hands are full of these.

22. There is joy in the setting-out; there is joy in the journey; there is joy in the goal.

23. Only if ye are sorrowful, or weary, or angry, or discomforted; then ye may know that ye have lost the golden thread, the thread wherewith I guide you to the heart of the groves of Eleusis.

24. My disciples are proud and beautiful; they are strong and swift; they rule their way like mighty conquerors.

25. The weak, the timid, the imperfect, the cowardly, the poor, the tearful—these are mine enemies, and I am come to destroy them.

26. This also is compassion: an end to the sickness of earth. A rooting-out of the weeds: a watering of the flowers.

27. O my children, ye are more beautiful than the flowers: ye must not fade in your season.

28. I love you; I would sprinkle you with the divine dew of immortality.

29. This immortality is no vain hope beyond the grave: I offer you the certain consciousness of bliss.

30. I offer it at once, on earth; before an hour hath struck upon the bell, ye shall be with Me in the Abodes that are beyond Decay.

31. Also I give you power earthly and joy earthly; wealth, and health, and length of days. Adoration and love shall cling to your feet, and twine around your heart.

32. Only your mouths shall drink of a delicious wine—the wine of Iacchus; they shall reach ever to the heavenly kiss of the Beautiful God.

33. I reveal unto you a great mystery. Ye stand between the abyss of height and the abyss of depth.

34. In either awaits you a Companion; and that Companion is Yourself.

35. Ye can have no other Companion.

36. Many have arisen, being wise. They have said « Seek out the glittering Image in the place ever golden, and unite yourselves with It. »

37. Many have arisen, being foolish. They have said, « Stoop down unto the darkly splendid world, and be wedded to that Blind Creature of the Slime. »

38. I who am beyond Wisdom and Folly, arise and say unto you: achieve both weddings! Unite yourselves with both!

39. Beware, beware, I say, lest ye seek after the one and lose the other!

40. My adepts stand upright; their head above the heavens, their feet below the hells.

41. But since one is naturally attracted to the Angel, another to the Demon, let the first strengthen the lower link, the last attach more firmly to the higher.

42. Thus shall equilibrium become perfect. I will aid my disciples; as fast as they acquire this balanced power and joy so faster will I push them.

43. They shall in their turn speak from this Invisible Throne; their words shall illumine the worlds.

44. They shall be masters of majesty and might; they shall be beautiful and joyous; they shall be clothed with victory and splendour; they shall stand upon the firm foundation; the kingdom shall be theirs; yea, the kingdom shall be theirs.

In the name of the Lord of Initiation. Amen.

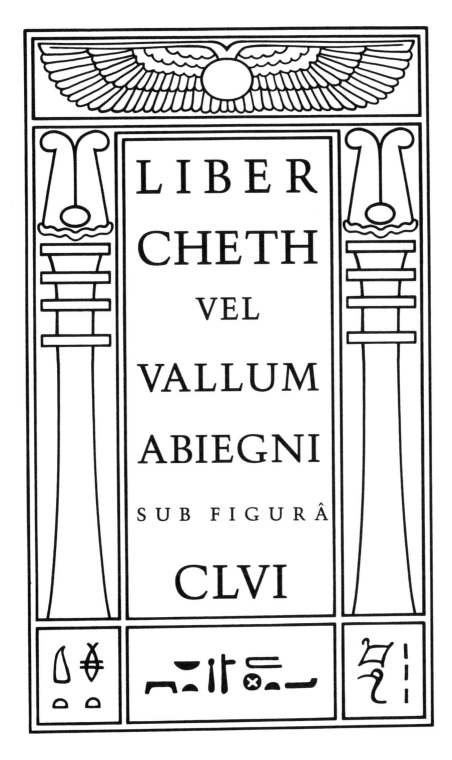

# LIBER CHETH

## VEL

# VALLUM

# ABIEGNI

### SUB FIGURÂ

# CLVI

A∴A∴
Publication in Class A.

1. This is the secret of the Holy Graal, that is the sacred vessel of our Lady the Scarlet Woman, Babalon the Mother of Abominations, the bride of Chaos, that rideth upon our Lord the Beast.
2. Thou shalt drain out thy blood that is thy life into the golden cup of her fornication.
3. Thou shalt mingle thy life with the universal life. Thou shalt keep not back one drop.
4. Then shall thy brain be dumb, and thy heart beat no more, and all thy life shall go from thee; and thou shalt be cast out upon the midden, and the birds of the air shall feast upon thy flesh, and thy bones shall whiten in the sun.
5. Then shall the winds gather themselves together, and bear thee up as it were a little heap of dust in a sheet that hath four corners, and they shall give it unto the guardians of the abyss.
6. And because there is no life therein, the guardians of the abyss shall bid the angels of the winds pass by. And the angels shall lay thy dust in the City of the Pyramids, and the name thereof shall be no more.
7. Now therefore that thou mayest achieve this ritual of the Holy Graal, do thou divest thyself of all thy goods.
8. Thou hast wealth; give it unto them that have need thereof, yet no desire toward it.
9. Thou hast health; slay thyself in the fervour of thine abandonment unto Our Lady. Let thy flesh hang loose

upon thy bones, and thine eyes glare with thy quenchless lust unto the Infinite, with thy passion for the Unknown, for Her that is beyond Knowledge the accursèd one.

10. Thou hast love; tear thy mother from thine heart, and spit in the face of thy father. Let thy foot trample the belly of thy wife, and let the babe at her breast be the prey of dogs and vultures.

11. For if thou dost not this with thy will, then shall We do this despite thy will. So that thou attain to the Sacrament of the Graal in the Chapel of Abominations.

12. And behold! if by stealth thou keep unto thyself one thought of thine, then shalt thou be cast out into the abyss for ever; and thou shalt be the lonely one, the eater of dung, the afflicted in the Day of Be-with-Us.

13. Yea! verily this is the Truth, this is the Truth, this is the Truth. Unto thee shall be granted joy and health and wealth and wisdom when thou art no longer thou.

14. Then shall every gain be a new sacrament, and it shall not defile thee; thou shalt revel with the wanton in the market-place, and the virgins shall fling roses upon thee, and the merchants bend their knees and bring thee gold and spices. Also young boys shall pour wonderful wines for thee, and the singers and the dancers shall sing and dance for thee.

15. Yet shalt thou not be therein, for thou shalt be forgotten, dust lost in dust.

16. Nor shall the æon itself avail thee in this; for from the dust shall a white ash be prepared by Hermes the Invisible.

17. And this is the wrath of God, that these things should be thus.

18. And this is the grace of God, that these things should be thus.

19. Wherefore I charge you that ye come unto me in the Beginning; for if ye take but one step in this Path, ye must arrive inevitably at the end thereof.

20. This Path is beyond Life and Death; it is also beyond Love; but that ye know not, for ye know not Love.

21. And the end thereof is known not even unto Our Lady or to the Beast whereon She rideth; nor unto the Virgin her daughter nor unto Chaos her lawful Lord; but unto the Crowned Child is it known? It is not known if it be known.

22. Therefore unto Hadit and unto Nuit be the glory in the End and the Beginning; yea, in the End and the Beginning.

LIBER
AL VEL
LEGIS

SUB FIGURÂ

CCXX

AS DELIVERED BY

XCIII = 418

TO

DCLXVI

A∴A∴
Publication in Class A.

1. Had!  The manifestation of Nuit.
2. The unveiling of the company of heaven.
3. Every man and every woman is a star.
4. Every number is infinite; there is no difference.
5. Help me, o warrior lord of Thebes, in my unveiling before the Children of men!
6. Be thou Hadit, my secret centre, my heart & my tongue!
7. Behold! it is revealed by Aiwass the minister of Hoor-paar-kraat.
8. The Khabs is in the Khu, not the Khu in the Khabs.
9. Worship then the Khabs, and behold my light shed over you!
10. Let my servants be few & secret: they shall rule the many & the known.
11. These are fools that men adore; both their Gods & their men are fools.
12. Come forth, o children, under the stars, & take your fill of love!
13. I am above you and in you.  My ecstasy is in yours. My joy is to see your joy.
14. Above, the gemmèd azure is
       The naked splendour of Nuit;
   She bends in ecstasy to kiss
       The secret ardours of Hadit.
   The wingèd globe, the starry blue,
   Are mine, O Ankh-af-na-khonsu!

15. Now ye shall know that the chosen priest & apostle of infinite space is the prince-priest the Beast; and in his woman called the Scarlet Woman is all power given. They shall gather my children into their fold: they shall bring the glory of the stars into the hearts of men.

16. For he is ever a sun, and she a moon. But to him is the winged secret flame, and to her the stooping starlight.

17. But ye are not so chosen.

18. Burn upon their brows, o splendrous serpent!

19. O azure-lidded woman, bend upon them!

20. The key of the rituals is in the secret word which I have given unto him.

21. With the God & the Adorer I am nothing: they do not see me. They are as upon the earth; I am Heaven, and there is no other God than me, and my lord Hadit.

22. Now, therefore, I am known to ye by my name Nuit, and to him by a secret name which I will give him when at last he knoweth me. Since I am Infinite Space, and the Infinite Stars thereof, do ye also thus. Bind nothing! Let there be no difference made among you between any one thing & any other thing; for thereby there cometh hurt.

23. But whoso availeth in this, let him be the chief of all!

24. I am Nuit, and my word is six and fifty.

25. Divide, add, multiply, and understand.

26. Then saith the prophet and slave of the beauteous one: Who am I, and what shall be the sign? So she answered him, bending down, a lambent flame of blue, all-touching, all penetrant, her lovely hands upon the black earth, & her lithe body arched for love, and her soft feet not hurting the little flowers: Thou knowest! And the sign shall be my ecstasy, the consciousness of the continuity of existence, the omnipresence of my body.

27. Then the priest answered & said unto the Queen of Space, kissing her lovely brows, and the dew of her light bathing his whole body in a sweet-smelling perfume of sweat: O Nuit, continuous one of Heaven, let it be ever thus; that men speak not of Thee as One but as None; and let them speak not of thee at all, since thou art continuous!

28. None, breathed the light, faint & færy, of the stars, and two.

29. For I am divided for love's sake, for the chance of union.

30. This is the creation of the world, that the pain of division is as nothing, and the joy of dissolution all.

31. For these fools of men and their woes care not thou at all! They feel little; what is, is balanced by weak joys; but ye are my chosen ones.

32. Obey my prophet! follow out the ordeals of my knowledge! seek me only! Then the joys of my love will redeem ye from all pain. This is so: I swear it by the vault of my body; by my sacred heart and tongue; by all I can give, by all I desire of ye all.

33. Then the priest fell into a deep trance or swoon, & said unto the Queen of Heaven; Write unto us the ordeals; write unto us the rituals; write unto us the law!

34. But she said: the ordeals I write not: the rituals shall be half known and half concealed: the Law is for all.

35. This that thou writest is the threefold book of Law.

36. My scribe Ankh-af-na-khonsu, the priest of the princes, shall not in one letter change this book; but lest there be folly, he shall comment thereupon by the wisdom of Ra-Hoor-Khu-it.

37. Also the mantras and spells; the obeah and the wanga; the work of the wand and the work of the sword; these he shall learn and teach.

38. He must teach; but he may make severe the ordeals.

39. The word of the Law is Θελημα.

40. Who calls us Thelemites will do no wrong, if he look but close into the word. For there are therein Three Grades, the Hermit, and the Lover, and the man of Earth. Do what thou wilt shall be the whole of the Law.

41. The word of Sin is Restriction. O man! refuse not thy wife, if she will! O lover, if thou wilt, depart! There is no bond that can unite the divided but love: all else is a curse. Accursèd! Accursèd be it to the æons! Hell.

42. Let it be that state of manyhood bound and loathing. So with thy all; thou hast no right but to do thy will.

43. Do that, and no other shall say nay.

44. For pure will, unassuaged of purpose, delivered from the lust of result, is every way perfect.

45. The Perfect and the Perfect are one Perfect and not two; nay, are none!

46. Nothing is a secret key of this law. Sixty-one the Jews call it; I call it eight, eighty, four hundred & eighteen.

47. But they have the half: unite by thine art so that all disappear.

48. My prophet is a fool with his one, one, one; are not they the Ox, and none by the Book?

49. Abrogate are all rituals, all ordeals, all words and signs. Ra-Hoor-Khuit hath taken his seat in the East at the Equinox of the Gods; and let Asar be with Isa, who also are one. But they are not of me. Let Asar be the adorant, Isa the sufferer; Hoor in his secret name and splendour is the Lord initiating.

50. There is a word to say about the Hierophantic task. Behold! there are three ordeals in one, and it may be given in three ways. The gross must pass through fire; let the fine be tried in intellect, and the lofty chosen ones

in the highest. Thus ye have star & star, system & system; let not one know well the other!

51. There are four gates to one palace; the floor of that palace is of silver and gold; lapis lazuli & jasper are there; and all rare scents; jasmine & rose, and the emblems of death. Let him enter in turn or at once the four gates; let him stand on the floor of the palace. Will he not sink? Amn. Ho! warrior, if thy servant sink? But there are means and means. Be goodly therefore: dress ye all in fine apparel; eat rich foods and drink sweet wines and wines that foam! Also, take your fill and will of love as ye will, when, where and with whom ye will! But always unto me.

52. If this be not aright; if ye confound the space-marks, saying: They are one; or saying, They are many; if the ritual be not ever unto me: then expect the direful judgments of Ra Hoor Khuit!

53. This shall regenerate the world, the little world my sister, my heart & my tongue, unto whom I send this kiss. Also, o scribe and prophet, though thou be of the princes, it shall not assuage thee nor absolve thee. But ecstasy be thine and joy of earth: ever To me! To me!

54. Change not as much as the style of a letter; for behold! thou, o prophet, shalt not behold all these mysteries hidden therein.

55. The child of thy bowels, *he* shall behold them.

56. Expect him not from the East, nor from the West; for from no expected house cometh that child. Aum! All words are sacred and all prophets true; save only that they understand a little; solve the first half of the equation, leave the second unattacked. But thou hast all in the clear light, and some, though not all, in the dark.

57. Invoke me under my stars! Love is the law, love under will. Nor let the fools mistake love; for there are love

and love. There is the dove, and there is the serpent. Choose ye well! He, my prophet, hath chosen, knowing the law of the fortress, and the great mystery of the House of God.

All these old letters of my Book are aright; but ⋖ is not the Star. This also is secret: my prophet shall reveal it to the wise.

58. I give unimaginable joys on earth: certainty, not faith, while in life, upon death; peace unutterable, rest, ecstasy; nor do I demand aught in sacrifice.

59. My incense is of resinous woods & gums; and there is no blood therein: because of my hair the trees of Eternity.

60. My number is 11, as all their numbers who are of us. The Five Pointed Star, with a Circle in the Middle, & the circle is Red. My colour is black to the blind, but the blue & gold are seen of the seeing. Also I have a secret glory for them that love me.

61. But to love me is better than all things: if under the night-stars in the desert thou presently burnest mine incense before me, invoking me with a pure heart, and the Serpent flame therein, thou shalt come a little to lie in my bosom. For one kiss wilt thou then be willing to give all; but whoso gives one particle of dust shall lose all in that hour. Ye shall gather goods and store of women and spices; ye shall wear rich jewels; ye shall exceed the nations of the earth in splendour & pride; but always in the love of me, and so shall ye come to my joy. I charge you earnestly to come before me in a single robe, and covered with a rich headdress. I love you! I yearn to you! Pale or purple, veiled or voluptuous, I who am all pleasure and purple, and drunkenness of the innermost sense, desire you. Put on

the wings, and arouse the coiled splendour within you: come unto me!

62. At all my meetings with you shall the priestess say—and her eyes shall burn with desire as she stands bare and rejoicing in my secret temple—To me! To me! calling forth the flame of the hearts of all in her love-chant.

63. Sing the rapturous love-song unto me! Burn to me perfumes! Wear to me jewels! Drink to me, for I love you! I love you!

64. I am the blue-lidded daughter of Sunset; I am the naked brilliance of the voluptuous night-sky.

65. To me! To me!

66. The Manifestation of Nuit is at an end.

1. Nu! the hiding of Hadit.
2. Come! all ye, and learn the secret that hath not yet been revealed. I, Hadit, am the complement of Nu, my bride. I am not extended, and Khabs is the name of my House.
3. In the sphere I am everywhere the centre, as she, the circumference, is nowhere found.
4. Yet she shall be known & I never.
5. Behold! the rituals of the old time are black. Let the evil ones be cast away; let the good ones be purged by the prophet! Then shall this Knowledge go aright.
6. I am the flame that burns in every heart of man, and in the core of every star. I am Life, and the giver of Life, yet therefore is the knowledge of me the knowledge of death.
7. I am the Magician and the Exorcist. I am the axle of the wheel, and the cube in the circle. « Come unto me » is a foolish word: for it is I that go.
8. Who worshipped Heru-pa-kraath have worshipped me; ill, for I am the worshipper.
9. Remember all ye that existence is pure joy; that all the sorrows are but as shadows; they pass & are done; but there is that which remains.
10. O prophet! thou hast ill will to learn this writing.
11. I see thee hate the hand & the pen; but I am stronger.
12. Because of me in Thee which thou knewest not.

13. for why? Because thou wast the knower, and me.

14. Now let there be a veiling of this shrine: now let the light devour men and eat them up with blindness!

15. For I am perfect, being Not; and my number is nine by the fools; but with the just I am eight, and one in eight: Which is vital, for I am none indeed. The Empress and the King are not of me; for there is a further secret.

16. I am The Empress & the Hierophant. Thus eleven, as my bride is eleven.

17. Hear me, ye people of sighing!
    The sorrows of pain and regret
Are left to the dead and the dying,
    The folk that not know me as yet.

18. These are dead, these fellows; they feel not. We are not for the poor and sad: the lords of the earth are our kinsfolk.

19. Is a God to live in a dog? No! but the highest are of us. They shall rejoice, our chosen: who sorroweth is not of us.

20. Beauty and strength, leaping laughter and delicious languor, force and fire, are of us.

21. We have nothing with the outcast and the unfit: let them die in their misery. For they feel not. Compassion is the vice of kings: stamp down the wretched & the weak: this is the law of the strong: this is our law and the joy of the world. Think not, o king, upon that lie: That Thou Must Die: verily thou shalt not die, but live. Now let it be understood: If the body of the King dissolve, he shall remain in pure ecstasy for ever. Nuit! Hadit! Ra-Hoor-Khuit! The Sun, Strength & Sight, Light; these are for the servants of the Star & the Snake.

22. I am the Snake that giveth Knowledge & Delight and

bright glory, and stir the hearts of men with drunkenness. To worship me take wine and strange drugs whereof I will tell my prophet, & be drunk thereof! They shall not harm ye at all. It is a lie, this folly against self. The exposure of innocence is a lie. Be strong, o man! lust, enjoy all things of sense and rapture: fear not that any God shall deny thee for this.

23. I am alone: there is no God where I am.

24. Behold! these be grave mysteries; for there are also of my friends who be hermits. Now think not to find them in the forest or on the mountain; but in beds of purple, caressed by magnificent beasts of women with large limbs, and fire and light in their eyes, and masses of flaming hair about them; there shall ye find them. Ye shall see them at rule, at victorious armies, at all the joy; and there shall be in them a joy a million times greater than this. Beware lest any force another, King against King! Love one another with burning hearts; on the low men trample in the fierce lust of your pride, in the day of your wrath.

25. Ye are against the people, O my chosen!

26. I am the secret Serpent coiled about to spring: in my coiling there is joy. If I lift up my head, I and my Nuit are one. If I droop down mine head, and shoot forth venom, then is rapture of the earth, and I and the earth are one.

27. There is great danger in me; for who doth not understand these runes shall make a great miss. He shall fall down into the pit called Because, and there he shall perish with the dogs of Reason.

28. Now a curse upon Because and his kin!

29. May Because be accursèd for ever!

30. If Will stops and cries Why, invoking Because, then Will stops & does nought.

31. If Power asks why, then is Power weakness.
32. Also reason is a lie; for there is a factor infinite & unknown; & all their words are skew-wise.
33. Enough of Because! Be he damned for a dog!
34. But ye, o my people, rise up & awake!
35. Let the rituals be rightly performed with joy & beauty!
36. There are rituals of the elements and feasts of the times.
37. A feast for the first night of the Prophet and his Bride!
38. A feast for the three days of the writing of the Book of the Law.
39. A feast for Tahuti and the child of the Prophet—secret, O Prophet!
40. A feast for the Supreme Ritual, and a feast for the Equinox of the Gods.
41. A feast for fire and a feast for water; a feast for life and a greater feast for death!
42. A feast every day in your hearts in the joy of my rapture!
43. A feast every night unto Nu, and the pleasure of uttermost delight!
44. Aye! feast! rejoice! there is no dread hereafter. There is the dissolution, and eternal ecstasy in the kisses of Nu.
45. There is death for the dogs.
46. Dost thou fail? Art thou sorry? Is fear in thine heart?
47. Where I am these are not.
48. Pity not the fallen! I never knew them. I am not for them. I console not: I hate the consoled & the consoler.
49. I am unique & conqueror. I am not of the slaves that perish. Be they damned & dead! Amen. (This is of the 4: there is a fifth who is invisible, & therein am I as a babe in an egg.)
50. Blue am I and gold in the light of my bride: but the red gleam is in my eyes; & my spangles are purple & green.

51. Purple beyond purple: it is the light higher than eyesight.

52. There is a veil: that veil is black. It is the veil of the modest woman; it is the veil of sorrow, & the pall of death: this is none of me. Tear down that lying spectre of the centuries: veil not your vices in virtuous words: these vices are my service; ye do well, & I will reward you here and hereafter.

53. Fear not, o prophet, when these words are said, thou shalt not be sorry. Thou art emphatically my chosen; and blessed are the eyes that thou shalt look upon with gladness. But I will hide thee in a mask of sorrow: they that see thee shall fear thou art fallen: but I lift thee up.

54. Nor shall they who cry aloud their folly that thou meanest nought avail; thou shall reveal it: thou availest: they are the slaves of because: They are not of me. The stops as thou wilt; the letters? change them not in style or value!

55. Thou shalt obtain the order & value of the English Alphabet; thou shalt find new symbols to attribute them unto.

56. Begone! ye mockers; even though ye laugh in my honour ye shall laugh not long: then when ye are sad know that I have forsaken you.

57. He that is righteous shall be righteous still; he that is filthy shall be filthy still.

58. Yea! deem not of change: ye shall be as ye are, & not other. Therefore the kings of the earth shall be Kings for ever: the slaves shall serve. There is none that shall be cast down or lifted up: all is ever as it was. Yet there are masked ones my servants: it may be that yonder beggar is a King. A King may choose his garment as he will: there is no certain test: but a beggar cannot hide his poverty.

59. Beware therefore! Love all, lest perchance is a King

concealed! Say you so? Fool! If he be a King, thou canst not hurt him.

60. Therefore strike hard & low, and to hell with them, master!

61. There is a light before thine eyes, o prophet, a light undesired, most desirable.

62. I am uplifted in thine heart; and the kisses of the stars rain hard upon thy body.

63. Thou art exhaust in the voluptuous fullness of the inspiration; the expiration is sweeter than death, more rapid and laughterful than a caress of Hell's own worm.

64. Oh! thou art overcome: we are upon thee; our delight is all over thee: hail! hail: prophet of Nu! prophet of Had! prophet of Ra-Hoor-Khu! Now rejoice! now come in our splendour & rapture! Come in our passionate peace, & write sweet words for the Kings!

65. I am the Master: thou art the Holy Chosen One.

66. Write, & find ecstasy in writing! Work, & be our bed in working! Thrill with the joy of life & death! Ah! thy death shall be lovely: whoso seeth it shall be glad. Thy death shall be the seal of the promise of our agelong love. Come! lift up thine heart & rejoice! We are one; we are none.

67. Hold! Hold! Bear up in thy rapture; fall not in swoon of the excellent kisses!

68. Harder! Hold up thyself! Lift thine head! breathe not so deep—die!

69. Ah! Ah! What do I feel? Is the word exhausted?

70. There is help & hope in other spells. Wisdom says: be strong! Then canst thou bear more joy. Be not animal; refine thy rapture! If thou drink, drink by the eight and ninety rules of art: if thou love, exceed by delicacy; and if thou do aught joyous, let there be subtlety therein!

71. But exceed! exceed!

72. Strive ever to more! and if thou art truly mine—and doubt it not, an if thou art ever joyous!—death is the crown of all.

73. Ah! Ah! Death! Death! thou shalt long for death. Death is forbidden, o man, unto thee.

74. The length of thy longing shall be the strength of its glory. He that lives long & desires death much is ever the King among the Kings.

75. Aye! listen to the numbers & the words:

76. 4 6 3 8 A B K 2 4 A L G M O R 3 Y X 24 89 R P S T O V A L. What meaneth this, o prophet? Thou knowest not; nor shalt thou know ever. There cometh one to follow thee: he shall expound it. But remember, o chosen one, to be me; to follow the love of Nu in the star-lit heaven; to look forth upon men, to tell them this glad word.

77. O be thou proud and mighty among men!

78. Lift up thyself! for there is none like unto thee among men or among Gods! Lift up thyself, o my prophet, thy stature shall surpass the stars. They shall worship thy name, foursquare, mystic, wonderful, the number of the man; and the name of thy house 418.

79. The end of the hiding of Hadit; and blessing & worship to the prophet of the lovely Star!

1. Abrahadabra; the reward of Ra Hoor Khut.
2. There is division hither homeward; there is a word not known. Spelling is defunct; all is not aught. Beware! Hold! Raise the spell of Ra-Hoor-Khuit!
3. Now let it be first understood that I am a god of War and of Vengeance. I shall deal hardly with them.
4. Choose ye an island!
5. Fortify it!
6. Dung it about with enginery of war!
7. I will give you a war-engine.
8. With it ye shall smite the peoples; and none shall stand before you.
9. Lurk! Withdraw! Upon them! this is the Law of the Battle of Conquest: thus shall my worship be about my secret house.
10. Get the stélé of revealing itself; set it in thy secret temple—and that temple is already aright disposed—& it shall be your Kiblah for ever. It shall not fade, but miraculous colour shall come back to it day after day. Close it in locked glass for a proof to the world.
11. This shall be your only proof. I forbid argument. Conquer! That is enough. I will make easy to you the abstraction from the ill-ordered house in the Victorious City. Thou shalt thyself convey it with worship, o prophet, though thou likest it not. Thou shalt have danger & trouble. Ra-Hoor-Khu is with thee. Worship me with fire & blood; worship me with swords & with spears. Let the woman be girt with a sword before

121

me: let blood flow to my name. Trample down the Heathen; be upon them, o warrior, I will give you of their flesh to eat!

12. Sacrifice cattle, little and big: after a child.

13. But not now.

14. Ye shall see that hour, o blessèd Beast, and thou the Scarlet Concubine of his desire!

15. Ye shall be sad thereof.

16. Deem not too eagerly to catch the promises; fear not to undergo the curses. Ye, even ye, know not this meaning all.

17. Fear not at all; fear neither men nor Fates, nor gods, nor anything. Money fear not, nor laughter of the folk folly, nor any other power in heaven or upon the earth or under the earth. Nu is your refuge as Hadit your light; and I am the strength, force, vigour, of your arms.

18. Mercy let be off: damn them who pity! Kill and torture; spare not; be upon them!

19. That stélé they shall call the Abomination of Desolation; count well its name, & it shall be to you as 718.

20. Why? Because of the fall of Because, that he is not there again.

21. Set up my image in the East: thou shalt buy thee an image which I will show thee, especial, not unlike the one thou knowest. And it shall be suddenly easy for thee to do this.

22. The other images group around me to support me: let all be worshipped, for they shall cluster to exalt me. I am the visible object of worship; the others are secret; for the Beast & his Bride are they: and for the winners of the Ordeal x. What is this? Thou shalt know.

23. For perfume mix meal & honey & thick leavings of red wine: then oil of Abramelin and olive oil, and afterward soften & smooth down with rich fresh blood.

24. The best blood is of the moon, monthly: then the fresh blood of a child, or dropping from the host of heaven: then of enemies; then of the priest or of the worshippers: last of some beast, no matter what.

25. This burn: of this make cakes & eat unto me. This hath also another use; let it be laid before me, and kept thick with perfumes of your orison: it shall become full of beetles as it were and creeping things sacred unto me.

26. These slay, naming your enemies; & they shall fall before you.

27. Also these shall breed lust & power of lust in you at the eating thereof.

28. Also ye shall be strong in war.

29. Moreover, be they long kept, it is better; for they swell with my force. All before me.

30. My altar is of open brass work: burn thereon in silver or gold!

31. There cometh a rich man from the West who shall pour his gold upon thee.

32. From gold forge steel!

33. Be ready to fly or to smite!

34. But your holy place shall be untouched throughout the centuries: though with fire and sword it be burnt down & shattered, yet an invisible house there standeth, and shall stand until the fall of the Great Equinox; when Hrumachis shall arise and the double-wanded one assume my throne and place. Another prophet shall arise, and bring fresh fever from the skies; another woman shall awake the lust & worship of the Snake; another soul of God and beast shall mingle in the globèd priest; another sacrifice shall stain the tomb; another king shall reign; and blessing no longer be poured To the Hawk-headed mystical Lord!

35. The half of the word of Heru-ra-ha, called Hoor-pa-kraat and Ra-Hoor-Khut.

36. Then said the prophet unto the God:

37. I adore thee in the song—

> I am the Lord of Thebes, and I
>    The inspired forth-speaker of Mentu;
> For me unveils the veilèd sky,
>    The self-slain Ankh-af-na-khonsu
> Whose words are truth. I invoke, I greet
>    Thy presence, O Ra-Hoor-Khuit!
>
> Unity uttermost showed!
>    I adore the might of Thy breath,
> Supreme and terrible God,
>    Who makest the gods and death
> To tremble before Thee:—
>    I, I adore thee!
>
> Appear on the throne of Ra!
>    Open the ways of the Khu!
> Lighten the ways of the Ka!
>    The ways of the Khabs run through
> To stir me or still me!
>    Aum! let it fill me!

38. So that thy light is in me; & its red flame is as a sword in my hand to push thy order. There is a secret door that I shall make to establish thy way in all the quarters, (these are the adorations, as thou hast written), as it is said:

> The light is mine; its rays consume
>    Me: I have made a secret door
> Into the House of Ra and Tum,
>    Of Khephra and of Ahathoor.
> I am thy Theban, O Mentu,
>    The prophet Ankh-af-na-khonsu!

By Bes-na-Maut my breast I beat;
By wise Ta-Nech I weave my spell.
Show thy star-splendour, O Nuit!
Bid me within thine House to dwell,
O wingèd snake of light, Hadit!
Abide with me, Ra-Hoor-Khuit!

39. All this and a book to say how thou didst come hither and a reproduction of this ink and paper for ever—for in it is the word secret & not only in the English—and thy comment upon this the Book of the Law shall be printed beautifully in red ink and black upon beautiful paper made by hand; and to each man and woman that thou meetest, were it but to dine or to drink at them, it is the Law to give. Then they shall chance to abide in this bliss or no; it is no odds. Do this quickly!

40. But the work of the comment? That is easy; and Hadit burning in thy heart shall make swift and secure thy pen.

41. Establish at thy Kaaba a clerk-house: all must be done well and with business way.

42. The ordeals thou shalt oversee thyself, save only the blind ones. Refuse none, but thou shalt know & destroy the traitors. I am Ra-Hoor-Khuit; and I am powerful to protect my servant. Success is thy proof: argue not; convert not; talk not overmuch! Them that seek to entrap thee, to overthrow thee, them attack without pity or quarter; & destroy them utterly. Swift as a trodden serpent turn and strike! Be thou yet deadlier than he! Drag down their souls to awful torment: laugh at their fear: spit upon them!

43. Let the Scarlet Woman beware! If pity and compassion and tenderness visit her heart; if she leave my work to toy with old sweetnesses; then shall my vengeance be

known. I will slay me her child: I will alienate her heart: I will cast her out from men: as a shrinking and despised harlot shall she crawl through dusk wet streets, and die cold and an-hungered.

44. But let her raise herself in pride! Let her follow me in my way! Let her work the work of wickedness! Let her kill her heart! Let her be loud and adulterous! Let her be covered with jewels, and rich garments, and let her be shameless before all men!

45. Then will I lift her to pinnacles of power: then will I breed from her a child mightier than all the kings of the earth. I will fill her with joy: with my force shall she see & strike at the worship of Nu: she shall achieve Hadit.

46. I am the warrior Lord of the Forties: the Eighties cower before me, & are abased. I will bring you to victory & joy: I will be at your arms in battle & ye shall delight to slay. Success is your proof; courage is your armour; go on, go on, in my strength; & ye shall turn not back for any!

47. This book shall be translated into all tongues: but always with the original in the writing of the Beast; for in the chance shape of the letters and their position to one another: in these are mysteries that no Beast shall divine. Let him not seek to try: but one cometh after him, whence I say not, who shall discover the Key of it all. Then this line drawn is a key: then this circle squared in its failure is a key also. And Abrahadabra. It shall be his child & that strangely. Let him not seek after this; for thereby alone can he fall from it.

48. Now this mystery of the letters is done, and I want to go on to the holier place.

49. I am in a secret fourfold word, the blasphemy against all gods of men.

50. Curse them! Curse them! Curse them!

51. With my Hawk's head I peck at the eyes of Jesus as he hangs upon the cross.
52. I flap my wings in the face of Mohammed & blind him.
53. With my claws I tear out the flesh of the Indian and the Buddhist, Mongol and Din.
54. Bahlasti! Ompehda! I spit on your crapulous creeds.
55. Let Mary inviolate be torn upon wheels: for her sake let all chaste women be utterly despised among you!
56. Also for beauty's sake and love's!
57. Despise also all cowards; professional soldiers who dare not fight, but play; all fools despise!
58. But the keen and the proud, the royal and the lofty; ye are brothers!
59. As brothers fight ye!
60. There is no law beyond Do what thou wilt.
61. There is an end of the word of the God enthroned in Ra's seat, lightening the girders of the soul.
62. To Me do ye reverence! to me come ye through tribulation of ordeal, which is bliss.
63. The fool readeth this Book of the Law, and its comment; & he understandeth it not.
64. Let him come through the first ordeal, & it will be to him as silver.
65. Through the second, gold.
66. Through the third, stones of precious water.
67. Through the fourth, ultimate sparks of the intimate fire.
68. Yet to all it shall seem beautiful. Its enemies who say not so, are mere liars.
69. There is success.
70. I am the Hawk-Headed Lord of Silence & of Strength; my nemyss shrouds the night-blue sky.
71. Hail! ye twin warriors about the pillars of the world! for your time is nigh at hand.
72. I am the Lord of the Double Wand of Power; the wand

of the Force of Coph Nia—but my left hand is empty,
for I have crushed an Universe; & nought remains.

73. Paste the sheets from right to left and from top to
bottom: then behold!

74. There is a splendour in my name hidden and glorious,
as the sun of midnight is ever the son.

75. The ending of the words is the Word Abrahadabra.

The Book of the Law is Written

and Concealed.

Aum.   Ha.

# AL

## (LIBER LEGIS)

## THE BOOK OF THE LAW

## SUB FIGURÂ

# XXXI

AS DELIVERED BY
93 — AIWASS — 418
TO
ANKH-F-N-KHONSU
THE PRIEST OF THE
PRINCES WHO IS 666

A∴A∴

Publication in Class A.

Had! The manifestation of Nuit

The unveiling of the company of heaven

Every man and every woman is a star

Every number is infinite; there is no difference

Help me, o warrior lord of Thebes, in my unveiling before the Children of men

Be thou Hadit, my secret centre, my heart & my tongue.

Behold! it is revealed by Aiwass the minister of Hoor-paar-kraat

The Khabs is in the Khu, not the Khu in the Khabs

Worship then the Khabs, and behold my light shed over you.

131

2

Let my servants be few & secret : They shall
rule the many & the known.

There are fools that men adore ; both their
Gods & their men are fools.

Come forth, o children, under the stars
& take your fill of love . I am above you
and in you . My ecstasy is in yours My
joy is to see your joy

V 1. If Spell called the law.

Now ye shall know that the chosen
priest & apostle of infinite space is
the prince-priest the Beast and in

3

his woman, called The Scarlet Woman, is
all power given. They shall gather my
children into their fold: they shall bring the
glory of the stars into the hearts of men.
For he is ever a sun, and she a moon. But
to him is the winged secret flame and to
her the stooping starlight.
But ye are not so chosen
Burn upon their brows, o splendrous serpent!
O azure-lidded woman, bend upon them!
The key of the rituals is in the secret word
which I have given unto him

4

With the God & the Adorer I am nothing: they do not see me. They are as upon the earth I am Heaven, and there is no other God than me, and my lord Hadit.

Now therefore I am known to ye by my name Nuit, and to him by a secret name which I will give him when at last he knoweth me

Since I am Infinite Space and the Infinite Stars thereof, do ye also thus. Bind nothing! Let there be no difference made among you between any one thing & any

5

other thing; for thereby there cometh hurt.

But whoso availeth in this let him be
the chief of all!

I am Nuit and my word is six and fifty.

Divide, add, multiply and understand.

Then saith the prophet and slave of the
beauteous one. Who am I, and what shall
be the sign. So she answered him, bending
down, a lambent flame of blue, all-touching,
all penetrant, her lovely hands upon the
black earth & her lithe body arched for love
and her soft feet not hurting the

6

little flowers Thou knowest! And the sigh
shall be my ecstasy, the consciousness of
the continuity of existence, the ~~not~~
omnipresence of my body, ~~the in my momentary~~
~~has of mine fact of my involuntary~~

( ~~Finite this in whiter words~~ ) | One letter as
                               |   above.

( ~~But go further on~~ )

Then He first murmured & said unto
the Queen of Space, kissing her lovely brows
and the dew of her light bathing his whole
body in a sweet-smelling perfume of sweat
O Nuit, continuous one of Heaven, let it

7

be ever thus that men speak not of
Thee as One but as None and let
them speak not of thee at all since
thou art continuous.

None, breathed the light, faint & faery, of
the stars, and two. For I am divided
for love's sake, for the chance of union.
This is the creation of the world that
the pain of ~~distance~~ division is as nothing and
the joy of dissolution all.
For these fools of men and their

§

woes are not Thus at all! They feel
little; what is, is balanced by weak
joys: but ye are my chosen ones.

Obey my prophet! follow out the
ordeals of my knowledge! seek me
only! Then the joys of my love will
redeem ye from all pain. This is
so: I swear it by the vault of my
body; by my sacred heart and tongue;
by all I can give, by all I desire of
ye all.

Then the priest fell into a deep trance or

9

swoon & said unto The Queen of Heaven

Write unto us the ordeals write unto
us the rituals write unto us the law.

But she said the ordeals I write not
the rituals shall be half known and
half concealed : the law is for all

This That thou writest is the threefold
book of Law

My scribe Ankh-af-na-khonsu the
priest of the princes shall not in one
letter change this work ; but lest there
be folly, he shall comment thereupon
by the wisdom of Ra-Hoor-Khu-it.

10

Also the mantras and spells; the
obeah and the wanga; the work of
the wand and the work of the
sword: these he shall learn and teach.

He must teach; but he may make severe
the ordeals.

The word of the Law is Θελημα.

Who calls us Thelemites will do no
wrong, if he look but close into the
word. For there are therein Three
Grades, the Hermit and the Lover and
the man of Earth. Do what thou wilt

11

shall be the whole of the Law.

The word of Sin is Restriction. O man!
refuse not thy wife if she will. O
lover, if thou wilt, depart. There is
no bond that can unite the divided but
love: all else is a curse. Accursèd!
accursèd! be it to the aeons. Hell.

Let it be that state of manyhood
bound and loathing. So with thy all
thou hast no right but to do thy will.
Do that and no other shall say nay.
For pure will, unassuaged of purpose,

12

delivered from the lust of result, is
every way perfect—
The Perfect and the Perfect are one
Perfect and not two; nay, are none!
Nothing is a secret key of this law
Sixty-one the Jews call it; I call it
Eight, eighty, fourhundred & eighteen.
But they have the half: unite by thine
art so that all disappear.
My prophet is a fool with his one one
one; are not they the Ox and none
by the Book.

13

Abrogate are all rituals, all ordeals, all
words and signs. Ra-Hoor-Khuit hath
taken his seat in the East at the Equinox
of the Gods and let Asar be with Isa
who also are one. But they are not of
me. Let Asar be the adorant, Isa the
sufferer; Hoor in his secret name and
splendour is the Lord initiating.
There is a word to say about the Hierophantic
task. Behold! there are three ordeals in
one, and it may be given in three ways.
The gross must pass through fire; let the

ne be tried in intellect, and the
lofty chosen ones in the highest. Thus
ye have star & star, system & system;
let not one know well the other.

There are four gates to one palace;
the floor of that palace is of silver and
gold; lapis lazuli & jasper are there, and
all rare scents jasmine & rose, and the
emblems of death. Let him enter in turn
or at once the four gates; let him stand
on the floor of the palace. Will he
not sink? Amn. Ho! warrior, if thy
servant sink? But there are means

15

and means. Be goodly therefore: dress ye
all in fine apparel; eat rich foods and
drink sweet wines and wines that foam.
~~but~~ Also, take your fill and will of
love as ye will, when, where and with
whom ye will. But always unto me.
If this be not aright; if ye confound
the space-marks, saying: They are one
or saying They are many; if the ritual
be not ever unto me: then expect
the dreadful judgments of Ra Hoor Khuit!
This shall regenerate the world, the little

16

world my sister, my heart & my tongue,
unto whom I send this kiss. Also, o
scribe and prophet—though thou be of the
princes it shall not assuage thee nor
absolve thee. But ecstasy be thine and
joy of earth: ever To me To me

Change not as much as the style
of a letter; for behold thou o prophet—
shalt not behold all these mysteries
hidden therein.
The child of thy bowels, he shall behold
them.
Expect him not from the East nor from

17

the West, for from no expected house cometh that child. Aum! All words are sacred and all prophets true; save only that they understand a little; solve the first half of the equation, leave the second unattacked. But thou hast all in the clear light, and some, though not all, in the dark.

Invoke me under my stars. Love is the law, love under will. Nor let the fools mistake love; for there are love and love. There is the dove, and there is the serpent. Choose ye well! He, my prophet, hath

*18*

Chosen, knowing the law of the fortress
and the great mystery of the House of God

All these old letters of my Book are
aright; but ☙ is not the Star. This
also is secret: my prophet shall reveal
it to the wise.

I give unimaginable joys on earth: certainty,
not faith, while in life, upon death; peace
unutterable, rest, ecstasy: nor do I demand
aught in sacrifice.

My incense is of resinous woods & gums
and there is no blood therein: because of
my hair the trees of Eternity.

19

My number is 11, as all their numbers
who are of us. (Lost
                  Tolvery) My colour is flash & the
         the whole of my star is The two pointed star, with a
blind, but the blue & gold circle in the middle, & the circle is Red
                       are seen of the
seeing. Also I have a secret glory for
them that love me.

But to love me is better than all things: if
under the night-stars in the desert thou
presently burnest mine incense before me
invoking me with a pure heart and the
Serpent flame therein, then shalt come
a little- to lie in my bosom. For one kiss
wilt thou then be willing to give all:

20

But whoso gives one particle of dust
shall lose all in that hour. Ye shall
gather goods and store of women and
spices; ye shall wear rich jewels; ye
shall exceed the nations of the earth
in splendour & pride; but always in the
love of me, and so shall ye come to
my joy. I charge you earnestly to come
before me in a single robe and crowned
with a rich headdress. I love you I yearn to
you. Pale or purple, veiled or voluptuous, I
who am all pleasure and purple

21

and drunkenness of the innermost sense desire ye. Put on the wings and arouse the coiled splendour within you: come unto me At all my meetings with you shall the priestess say - and her eyes shall burn with desire as she stands bare and rejoicing in my secret temple - To me! To me! calling forth the flame of the hearts of all in her love - chant.

Sing the rapturous love - song unto me! Burn to me perfumes! Wear to me jewels! Drink to me, for I love you! I love you!

22.

I am the blue-lidded daughter of sunset; I am
the naked brilliance of the voluptuous night
sky

To me! To me!

The Manifestation of Nuit is at an
End.

*1*

1 Nu! the hiding of Hadit.

2 Come! all ye, and learn the secret that
hath not yet been revealed. I, Hadit am
the complement of Nu my bride. I am not
extended, and Khabs is the name of my House.

3 In the sphere I am everywhere, the centre, as
She, the circumference, is nowhere found.

4 Yet she shall be known & I never.

5 Behold! the rituals of the old time are black.
Let the evil ones be cast away; let the
good ones be purged by the prophet! Then shall
this Knowledge go aright.

6. I am the flame that burns in every heart of
man, and in the core of every star. I am

2

Life, and the giver of life; yet therefore is
the knowledge of me the knowledge of death.

7. I am the Magician and the Exorcist. I am the
axle of the wheel, and the cube in the circle.
"Come unto me" is a foolish word; for it is I that
go.

8 Who worshipped Heru-pa-kraath have
worshipped me; ill, for I am the worshipper.

9 Remember all ye that existence is pure joy;
that all the sorrows are but as shadows; they
pass & are done; but there is that which
remains.

10. O prophet! thou hast ill will to learn this
writing.

11. I see thee hate the hand & the pen; but I am

Stronger.

3

12 Because of me in Thee which thou knewest not.

13. for why? Because thou wast the knower, and me.

14. Now let there be a veiling of this shrine: now let the light devour men and eat them up with blindness.

15. For I am perfect, being Not; and my number is nine by the fools; but with the just I am Eight, and one in Eight: Which is vital, for I am none indeed. The Empress and the King are not of me; for there is a further secret.

16 I am the Empress & the Hierophant. Thus eleven, as my bride is eleven.

4

17) Hear me, ye people of sighing!
The sorrows of pain and regret
Are left to the dead and the dying,
The folk that not know me as yet.

18 These are dead, these fellows; they feel not. We
are not for the poor and sad: the lords of the
earth are our kinsfolk.

19 Is a God to live in a dog? No! but the
highest are of us. They shall rejoice, our chosen:
who sorroweth is not of us.

20 Beauty and strength, leaping laughter and
delicious languor, force and fire, are of us.

5

21 We have nothing with the outcast and the unfit:
let them die in their misery. For they feel
not. Compassion is the vice of kings: stamp
down the wretched & the weak: this is the
law of the strong: this is our law and the
joy of the world. Think not, o king, upon that
lie: That Thou Must Die: verily thou shalt
not die, but live! Now let it be understood
If the body of the King dissolve, he shall remain
in pure ecstasy for ever Nuit Hadit Ra-Hoor
Khuit. The Sun, Strength & Sight, Light; these
are for the servants of the Star & the Snake

6

22 I am the Snake that giveth Knowledge & Delight
and bright glory, and stir the hearts of men
with drunkenness. To worship me take wine
and strange drugs whereof I will tell my
prophet, & be drunk thereof! They shall not
harm ye at all. It is a lie, this folly
against self. The exposure of innocence
is a lie. Be strong, o man, lust, enjoy
all things of sense and rapture: fear not
that any God shall deny thee for this.
23 I am alone: there is no God where I am.
24 Behold! these be grave mysteries; for there
are also of my friends who be hermits. Now

Think not to find them in the forest or on the
mountain; but in beds of purple, caressed by
magnificent beasts of women with large limbs,
and fire and light in their eyes, and masses
of flaming hair about them; there shall ye
find them. Ye shall see them at rule, at
victorious armies, at all the joy; and there
shall be in them a joy a million times
greater than this. Beware lest any
force another, King against King! Love one
another with burning hearts; on the low men
trample in the fierce lust of your pride

8

in the day of your wrath.

25. Ye are against the people, O my chosen!

26. I am the secret Serpent coiled about to
spring: in my coiling there is joy. If I
lift up my head, I and my Nuit are one.
If I droop down mine head, and shoot
forth venom, then is rapture of the earth,
and I and the earth are one.

27. There is great danger in me; for who doth
not understand these runes shall make
a great miss. He shall fall down into
the pit called Because, and there he shall

9

reason with the dogs of Reason.

28 Now a curse upon Because and his kin!

29 May Because be accursèd for ever!

30 If Will stops and cries Why, invoking
Because, then Will stops & does nought.

31 If Power asks why, then is Power weakness.

32 Also reason is a lie; for there is a
factor infinite & unknown; & all their
words are skew-wise.

33 Enough of Because! Be he damned for a dog!

34. But ye, o my people, rise up & awake!

35. Let the rituals be rightly performed with
joy & beauty!

*10*

36 There are rituals of the elements and feasts
of the times.

37 A feast for the first night of the Prophet
and his Bride!

38 A feast for the three days of the writing of
the Book of the Law.

39 A feast for Tahuti and the child of the
Prophet — secret, O Prophet!

40 A feast for the Supreme Ritual, and a
feast for the Equinox of the Gods.

41 A feast for fire and a feast for water; a
feast for life and a greater feast for death!

*//*

42 A feast every day in your hearts in the joy of my rapture.

43 A feast every night unto Nuit, and the pleasure of uttermost delight.

44 Aye! feast! rejoice! there is no dread hereafter. There is the dissolution, and eternal ecstasy in the kisses of Nu.

45 There is death for the dogs.

46 Dost thou fail? Art thou sorry? Is fear in thine heart?

47 Where I am these are not.

12

48 Pity not the fallen! I never knew them.
I am not for them. I console not: I hate
the consoled & the consoler.

49 I am unique & conqueror. I am not of the
slaves that perish. Be they damned &
dead! Amen. [ This is of the 4: there is
a fifth who is invisible & therein am I
as a babe in an egg.]

50 Blue am I and gold in the light of my
bride: but the red gleam is in my eyes
& my spangles are purple & green.

51. Purple beyond purple: it is the light higher

13

than eyesight.

52 There is a veil: that veil is black. It is the veil of the modest woman; it is the veil of sorrow, & the pall of death: this is none of me. Tear down that lying spectre of the centuries: veil not your vices in virtuous words: these vices are my service; ye do well, & I will reward you here and hereafter.

53 Fear not, o prophet, when these words are said, thou shalt not be sorry. Thou art emphatically my chosen; and blessed are

14

the eyes that thou shalt look upon with
gladness. But I will hide thee in a
mask of sorrow: they that see thee shall
fear thou art fallen: but I lift thee up.

54 Nor shall they who cry aloud their folly
that thou meanest nought avail; thou
shall reveal it: thou availest: they are
the slaves of because: They are not of
me. The stops as thou wilt; the letters
change them not in style or value!

55 Thou shalt obtain the order & value of
the English Alphabet; thou shalt find

15

new symbols to attribute them unto.

56 Begone! ye mockers; even though ye laugh
in my honour ye shall laugh not long: then
when ye are sad know that I have
forsaken you.

57. He that is righteous shall be righteous still;
he that is filthy shall be filthy still.

58 Yea! deem not of change: ye shall be as ye
are, & not other. Therefore the kings of
the earth shall be kings for ever: the slaves
shall serve. There is none that shall
be cast down or lifted up: all is ever

16

as it was. Yet there are masked ones my
servants : it may be that yonder beggar is
a King. A King may choose his garment as
he will : there is no certain test : but a
beggar cannot hide his poverty.

59 Beware therefore ! Love all, lest perchance is a
King concealed ! Say you so? Fool! If he
be a King, thou canst not hurt him.

60 Therefore strike hard & low, and to hell
with them, master !

61 There is a light before thine eyes o prophet,
a light undesired, most desirable.

17

62 I am uplifted in thine heart and the kisses of the stars rain hard upon thy body.

63 Thou art exhaust in the voluptuous fullness of the aspiration: the aspiration is sweeter than death, more rapid and laughterful than a caress of Hell's own worm.

64 Oh! Thou art overcome: we are upon thee; our delight is all over thee; hail! hail! prophet of Nu! prophet of Had! prophet of Ra-Hoor-Khu! Now rejoice! now come in our splendour & rapture! Come in our passionate peace, & write sweet words for the Kings!

18

65 I am the Master: thou art the Holy Chosen One.

66 Write, & find ecstasy in writing! Work & be our bed in working! Thrill with the joy of life & death! Ah! thy death shall be lovely: whoso seeth it shall be glad. Thy death shall be the seal of the promise of our age long love. Come! lift up thine heart & rejoice! We are one; we are none.

67 Hold! Hold! Bear up in thy rapture; fall not in swoon of the excellent kisses!

68 Harder! Hold up thyself! Lift thine head!

19

breathe not so deep — die!

69 Ah! Ah! What do I feel? / / the word Exhausted?

70 There is help & hope in other spells. Wisdom says: be strong! Then canst thou bear more joy. Be not animal; refine thy rapture! If thou drink, drink by the eight and ninety rules of art: if thou love, exceed by delicacy; and if thou do aught joyous, let there be subtlety therein!

71 But exceed! exceed!

72 Strive ever to more! and if thou art truly

20

mine — and doubt it not, an if thou art
ever joyous! — death is the crown of all

33 Ah! I die! Death! Death! Thou shalt long for
death. Death is forbidden, o man, unto thee.

74 The length of thy longing shall be the strength
of its glory. He that lives long & desires
death much is ever the King among the Kings.

75 Aye! listen to the numbers & the words:

76   4 6 3 8 A B K 2 4 A L G M O R 3 Y
$\times \dfrac{2}{3}$ $\dfrac{8}{9}$ R P S T O V A L. What
meaneth this, o prophet? Thou knowest
not; nor shalt thou know ever. There
cometh one to follow thee: he shall

21

Expound it. But remember, o Chosen
one, to be me; to follow the love of
Nu in the star-lit heaven; to look forth
upon men, to tell them this glad word.

37 O be thou proud and mighty among men !

78 Lift up thyself! for there is none like unto
thee among men or among Gods ! Lift up
thyself, o my prophet, thy stature shall
surpass the stars They shall worship thy
name, foursquare, mystic, wonderful, the
number of the man; and the name of

22

thy house 418.

79 The end of the hiding of Hadit; and
blessing & worship to the prophet of
the lovely Star.

1

1 Abrahadabra! the reward of Ra Hoor Khut.

2 There is division hither homeward; there is a word not known. Spelling is defunct; all is not aught. Beware! Hold! Raise the spell of Ra-Hoor-Khuit.

3 Now let it be first understood that I am a god of War and of Vengeance. I shall deal hardly with them.

4 Choose ye an island!

5 Fortify it!

6 Dung it about with enginery of war!

7 I will give you a war-engine.

8 With it ye shall smite the peoples and

none shall stand before you.

2

9 Lurk! Withdraw! Upon them! This
is The Law of the Battle of Conquest: Thus
shall my worship be about my secret house.

10 Get the stélé of revealing itself; set it
in thy secret temple — and that temple
is already aright disposed — & it shall be your
Kiblah for ever. It shall not fade, but
miraculous colour shall come back to it
day after day. Close it in locked glass for a
proof to the world.

11 This shall be your only proof. I forbid argument.
Conquer! That is enough. I will make easy

3

to you the =abstraction= from the ill-ordered house in the Victorious City. Thou shalt thyself convey it with worship, o prophet, though thou likest it not. Thou shalt have danger & trouble. Ra-Hoor-Khu is with thee. Worship me with fire & blood; worship me with swords & with spears. Let the woman be girt with a sword before me: let blood flow to my name. Trample down the Heathen; be upon them, o warrior, I will give you of their flesh to eat!

12 Sacrifice cattle little and big: after a child.

4

13 But not now.

14 Ye shall see that hour, o blessed Beast, and thou the Scarlet Concubine of his desire!

15 Ye shall be sad thereof.

16 Deem not too eagerly to catch the promises; fear not to undergo the curses. Ye, even ye, know not this meaning all.

17 Fear not at all; fear neither men, nor Fates, nor gods, nor anything. Money fear not, nor laughter of the folk folly, nor any other power in heaven or upon the earth or under the earth. Nu is your refuge as Hadit your

5

light; and I am the strength, force, vigour of your arms.

18 Mercy let be off : damn them who pity. Kill and torture ; spare not ; be upon them.

19 That stélé they shall call the Abomination of Desolation; count well its name, & it shall be to you as 718.

20 Why? Because of the fall of Because, that he is not there again.

21 Set up my image in the East : thou shalt buy thee an image which I will show thee, especially not unlike the one thou knowest. And it shall be suddenly easy for thee to do this.

6

22. The other images group around me to support me: let all be worshipped, for they shall cluster to exalt me. I am the visible object of worship; the others are secret; for the Beast & his Bride are they: and for the winners of the Ordeal x. What is this? Thou shalt know.

23 For perfume mix meal & honey & thick leavings of red wine: then oil of Abramelin and olive oil, and afterward soften & smooth down with rich fresh blood!

24 The best blood is of the moon, monthly: then the fresh blood of a child, or dropping from the

7

host of heaven: then of enemies; then
of the priest or of the worshippers: last of
some beast, no matter what.

25 This burn: of this make cakes & eat unto
me. This hath also another use; let it be
laid before me, and kept thick with perfumes
of your orison: it shall become full of beetles
as it were and creeping things sacred unto me.

26 These slay, naming your enemies & they shall
fall before you.

27 Also these shall breed lust & power of lust in
you at the eating thereof.

28 Also ye shall be strong in war.

8

29 Moreover, be they long kept, it is better; for they swell with my force. All before me.

30 My altar is of open brass work: burn thereon in silver or gold.

31 There cometh a rich man from the West who shall pour his gold upon thee.

32 From gold forge steel:

33 Be ready to fly or to smite.

34 But your holy place shall be untouched throughout the centuries: though with fire and sword it be burnt down & shattered, yet an invisible house there standeth and shall stand until the fall of the Great

9

Equinox, when Hrumachis shall arise and
the double-wanded one assume my Throne and
place. Another prophet shall arise, and bring
fresh fever from the skies; another woman shall
wake the lust & worship of the Snake; another
soul of God and beast shall mingle in the
globéd priest; another sacrifice shall stain
the tomb; another king shall reign; and blessing
no longer be poured To the Hawk-headed
mystical Lord!

35 The half of the word of Heru-ra-ha, called
Hoor-pa-kraat and Ra-Hoor-Khut.

10

36 Then said the prophet unto the God.

37 " I adore thee in the song
" I am the Lord of Thebes" &c from Vellum book
———— " fill me

38 So that thy light is in me & its red flame
is as a sword in my hand to push thy
order. There is a secret door that I shall
make to establish thy way in all the quarters
(there are the adorations, as thou hast written)
as it is said

" The light is mine" &c
from vellum book. to " Ra - Hoor - Khuit "

11

39 All this and a book to say how thou
didst come hither and a reproduction of
this ink and paper for ever - for in it is
the word secret & not only in the English -
and they comment upon this the Book of the Law
shall be printed beautifully in red ink and
black upon beautiful paper made by hand;
and to each man and woman that thou
meetest, were it but to dine or to drink
at them, it is the Law to give. Then they
shall chance to abide in this bliss or no;
it is no odds. Do this quickly!

40 But the work of the comment? That is easy; and

12

Bandit. Cunning in My heart shall make swift and secure My pen.

41. Establish at thy Kaaba ~~at~~ a clerk-house: all must be done well and with a business way.

42. The ordeals thou shalt oversee thyself, save only the blind ones. Refuse none, but thou shalt know & destroy the traitors. I am Ra-Hoor-Khuit and I am powerful to protect my servant. Success is thy proof: argue not: convert not: talk not overmuch. Them that seek to entrap thee, to overthrow thee, them attack without pity or quarter; & destroy them utterly. Swift as a trodden serpent turn...

13

and strike! Be thou yet deadlier than he!

42 Drag down their souls to awful torment: laugh at their fear: spit upon them!

43 Let the Scarlet Woman beware! If pity and compassion and tenderness visit her heart if she leave my work to toy with old sweetnesses then shall my vengeance be known. I will slay me her child: I will alienate her heart: I will cast her out from men: as a shrinking and despised whore shall she crawl through dusk wet streets, and die cold and an-hungered.

14

44. But let her raise herself in pride. Let her follow me in my way. Let her work the work of wickedness! Let her kill her heart! Let her be loud and adulterous; let her be covered with jewels and rich garments, and let her be shameless before all men!

45 Then will I lift her to pinnacles of power: then will I breed from her a child mightier than all the kings of the earth. I will fill her with joy: with my force shall she see & strike at the worship of Nu. she shall achieve Hadit.

15

46. I am the warrior Lord of the Forties: the Eighties cower before me, & are abased. I will bring you to victory & joy: I will be at your arms in battle & ye shall delight to slay. Success is your proof; courage is your armour; go on, go on, in my strength & ye shall turn not back for any.

47. This book shall be translated into all tongues: but always with the original in the writing of the Beast; for in the

change in the shape of the letters and their
position to one another: in these are mysteries
that no Beast shall divine. Let him
not seek to try: but one cometh after
him, whence I say not, who shall
discover the Key of it all. Then
this line drawn is a key: then this
circle squared ⊕ in its failure is a
key also. And Abrahadabra. It shall
be his child & that strangely. Let him not
seek after this; for thereby alone can he
fall from it.

17

48 Now this mystery of the letters is done, and I want to go on to the holier place.

49 I am in a secret fourfold word the blasphemy against all gods of men.

50 Curse them! Curse them! Curse them!

51 With my Hawk's head I peck at the eyes of Jesus as he hangs upon the cross

52 I flap my wings in the face of Mohammed & blind him

53 With my claws I tear out the flesh of the Indian and the Buddhist, Mongol and Din.

54 Bahlasti! Ompehda! I spit on your

18

crapulous creeds.

55 Let Mary inviolate be torn upon wheels: for her sake let all chaste women be utterly despised among you.

56 Also for beauty's sake and love!

57 Despise also all cowards: professional soldiers who dare not fight, but play: all fools despise!

58 But the keen and the proud, the royal and the lofty: ye are brothers.

59 As brothers fight ye.

60 There is no law beyond Do what thou wilt.

61 There is an end of the word of the God

19

enthroned in Ra's seat, lightening the girders
of the soul.

62 To Me do ye reverence; to me come ye
through tribulation of ordeal, which is
bliss.

63 The fool readeth this Book of the Law, and
its comment & he understandeth it not.

64 Let him come through the first ordeal &
it will be to him as silver

65 Through the second gold

66 Through the third, stones of precious water.

67 Through the fourth, ultimate sparks of the
intimate fire.

20

68 Yet to all it shall seem beautiful. Its
enemies who say not so, are mere liars.

69 There is success

70 I am the Hawk-Headed Lord of Silence
& of Strength ; my nemyss shrouds the
night-blue sky.

71 Hail! ye twin warriors about the pillars of
the world! for your time is nigh at hand

72 I am the Lord of the Double Wand of Power
the wand of the ~~Force~~ Force of Coph Nia—I but my
left hand is empty, for I have crushed

21

an Universe & nought remains.

73 Paste the sheets from right to left and
from top to bottom: then behold!

74 There is a splendour in my name hidden
and glorious, as the sun of midnight is
ever the son

75 The ending of the words is the Word
Abrahadabra.

The Book of the Law is Written
and Concealed
Aum. Ha.

# THE COMMENT.

Do what thou wilt shall be the whole of the Law.

The study of this Book is forbidden. It is wise to destroy this copy after the first reading.

Whosoever disregards this does so at his own risk and peril. These are most dire.

Those who discuss the contents of this Book are to be shunned by all, as centres of pestilence.

All questions of the Law are to be decided only by appeal to my writings, each for himself.

There is no law beyond Do what thou wilt.

Love is the law, love under will.

The priest of the princes,

Ankh-f-n-khonsu

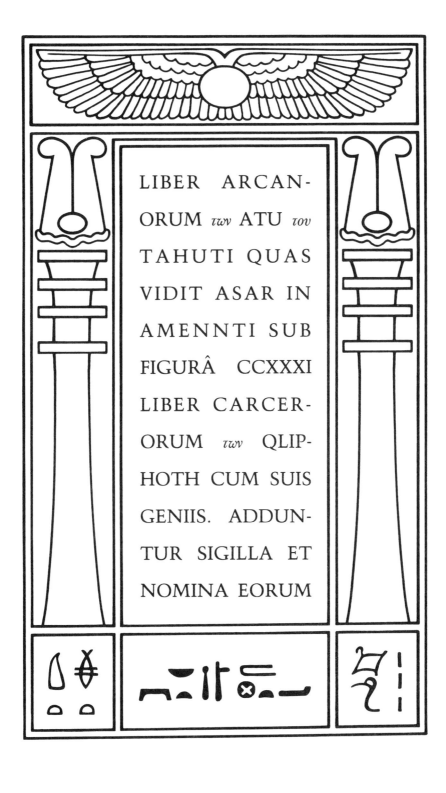

LIBER ARCAN-
ORUM *των* ATU *του*
TAHUTI QUAS
VIDIT ASAR IN
AMENNTI SUB
FIGURÂ CCXXXI
LIBER CARCER-
ORUM *των* QLIP-
HOTH CUM SUIS
GENIIS. ADDUN-
TUR SIGILLA ET
NOMINA EORUM

A∴A∴
Publication in Class A.

LIBER XXII CARCERORUM QLIPHOTH CUM SUIS GENIIS

Compare with

LIBER XXII DOMARUM MERCURII CUM SUIS GENIIS

199

(This book is true up to the grade of Adeptus Exemptus.
V.V.V.V.V. 8°, 3°.)

0. A, the heart of IAO, dwelleth in ecstasy in the secret place of the thunders. Between Asar and Asi he abideth in joy.
1. The lightnings increased and the Lord Tahuti stood forth. The Voice came from the Silence. Then the One ran and returned.
2. Now hath Nuit veiled herself, that she may open the gate of her sister.
3. The Virgin of God is enthroned upon an oyster-shell; she is like a pearl, and seeketh Seventy to her Four. In her heart is Hadit the invisible glory.
4. Now riseth Ra-Hoor-Khuit, and dominion is established in the Star of the Flame.
5. Also is the Star of the Flame exalted, bringing benediction to the universe.
6. Here then beneath the winged Eros is youth, delighting in the one and the other.

   He is Asar between Asi and Nepthi; he cometh forth from the veil.
7. He rideth upon the chariot of eternity; the white and the black are harnessed to his car. Therefore he reflecteth the Fool, and the sevenfold veil is reveiled.
8. Also came forth mother Earth with her lion, even Sekhet, the lady of Asi.
9. Also the Priest veiled himself, lest his glory be profaned, lest his word be lost in the multitude.
10. Now then the Father of all issued as a mighty wheel; the

Sphinx, and the dog-headed god, and Typhon, were bound on his circumference.

11. Also the lady Maat with her feather and her sword abode to judge the righteous.

For Fate was already established.

12. Then the holy one appeared in the great water of the North; as a golden dawn did he appear, bringing benediction to the fallen universe.

13. Also Asar was hidden in Amennti; and the Lords of Time swept over him with the sickle of death.

14. And a mighty angel appeared as a woman, pouring vials of woe upon the flames, lighting the pure stream with her brand of cursing. And the iniquity was very great.

15. Then the Lord Khem arose, He who is holy among the highest, and set up his crowned staff for to redeem the universe.

16. He smote the towers of wailing; he brake them in pieces in the fire of his anger, so that he alone did escape from the ruin thereof.

17. Transformed, the holy virgin appeared as a fluidic fire, making her beauty into a thunderbolt.

18. By her spells she invoked the Scarab, the Lord Kheph-Ra, so that the waters were cloven and the illusion of the towers was destroyed.

19. Then the sun did appear unclouded, and the mouth of Asi was on the mouth of Asar.

20. Then also the Pyramid was builded so that the Initiation might be complete.

21. And in the heart of the Sphinx danced the Lord Adonai, in His garlands of roses and pearls making glad the concourse of things; yea, making glad the concourse of things.

## THE GENII OF THE 22 SCALES OF THE SERPENT
## AND OF THE QLIPHOTH

| | | |
|---|---|---|
| א Aₑu-iao-uₑa [ₑ=ץ] . . . . | | Amprodias |
| ב Beₑθaoooabitom . . . . | | Baratchial |
| ג Gitωnosapφωllois . . . . | | Gargophias |
| ד Dηnaₛartarωθ [ₛ=st] . . . | | Dagdagiel |
| ה Hoo-oorω-iₛ . . . . . | | Hemethterith |
| ו Vuaretza — [a secret name follows] . | | Uriens |
| ז Zoowasar . . . . . | | Zamradiel |
| ח Chiva-abrahadabra-cadaxviii . . . | | Characith |
| ט Θalₑₛer-ā-dekerval . . . . | | Temphioth |
| י Iehuvahaₛanₑθatan . . . . | | Yamatu |
| כ Kerugunaviel . . . . | | Kurgasiax |
| ך Lusanaherandraton . . . . | | Lafcursiax |
| מ Malai . . . . . . | | Malkunofat |
| נ Nadimraphoroiozₑθalai . . . | | Niantiel |
| ם Salaθlala-amrodnaθₑiₛ . . . | | Saksaksalim |
| ע Oaoaaaoooₑ-iₛ . . . . | | A'ano'nin |
| פ Puraθmetai-apηmetai . . . . | | Parfaxitas |
| צ Xanθaₛeranϭϙ-iₛ [ϭϙ=sh, q] . . | | Tzuflifu |
| ק QaniΔnayx-ipamai . . . . | | Qulielfi |
| ר Ra-a-gioselahladnaimawa-iₛ . . . | | Raflifu |
| ש Shabnax-odobor . . . . | | Shalicu |
| ת Thath'th'thithₑthuth-thiₛ . . . | | Thantifaxath |

# LIBER A'ASH

VEL

CAPRICORNI

PNEUMATICI

SUB FIGURÂ

# CCCLXX

A∴A∴
Publication in Class A.

0. Gnarled Oak of God! In thy branches is the lightning nested! Above thee hangs the Eyeless Hawk.
1. Thou art blasted and black! Supremely solitary in that heath of scrub.
2. Up! The ruddy clouds hang over thee! It is the storm.
3. There is a flaming gash in the sky.
4. Up.
5. Thou art tossed about in the grip of the storm for an æon and an æon and an æon. But thou givest not thy sap; thou fallest not.
6. Only in the end shalt thou give up thy sap when the great God F. I. A. T. is enthroned on the day of Be-with-Us.
7. For two things are done and a third thing is begun. Isis and Osiris are given over to incest and adultery. Horus leaps up thrice armed from the womb of his mother. Harpocrates his twin is hidden within him. Set is his holy covenant, that he shall display in the great day of M. A. A. T., that is being interpreted the Master of the Temple of A.˙. A.˙., whose name is Truth.
8. Now in this is the magical power known.
9. It is like the oak that hardens itself and bears up against the storm. It is weather-beaten and scarred and confident like a sea-captain.
10. Also it straineth like a hound in the leash.
11. It hath pride and great subtlety. Yea, and glee also!
12. Let the magus act thus in his conjuration.
13. Let him sit and conjure; let him draw himself together

in that forcefulness; let him rise next swollen and straining; let him dash back the hood from his head and fix his basilisk eye upon the sigil of the demon. Then let him sway the force of him to and fro like a satyr in silence, until the Word burst from his throat.

14. Then let him not fall exhausted, although the might have been ten thousandfold the human; but that which floodeth him is the infinite mercy of the Genitor-Genetrix of the Universe, whereof he is the Vessel.

15. Nor do thou deceive thyself. It is easy to tell the live force from the dead matter. It is no easier to tell the live snake from the dead snake.

16. Also concerning vows. Be obstinate, and be not obstinate. Understand that the yielding of the Yoni is one with the lengthening of the Lingam. Thou art both these; and thy vow is but the rustling of the wind on Mount Meru.

17. Now shalt thou adore me who am the Eye and the Tooth, the Goat of the Spirit, the Lord of Creation. I am the Eye in the Triangle, the Silver Star that ye adore.

18. I am Baphomet, that is the Eightfold Word that shall be equilibrated with the Three.

19. There is no act or passion that shall not be a hymn in mine honour.

20. All holy things and all symbolic things shall be my sacraments.

21. These animals are sacred unto me; the goat, and the duck, and the ass, and the gazelle, the man, the woman and the child.

22. All corpses are sacred unto me; they shall not be touched save in mine eucharist. All lonely places are sacred unto me; where one man gathereth himself together in my name, there will I leap forth in the midst of him.

23. I am the hideous god; and who mastereth me is uglier than I.

24. Yet I give more than Bacchus and Apollo; my gifts exceed the olive and the horse.

25. Who worshippeth me must worship me with many rites.

26. I am concealed with all concealments; when the Most Holy Ancient One is stripped and driven through the marketplace I am still secret and apart.

27. Whom I love I chastise with many rods.

28. All things are sacred to me; no thing is sacred from me.

29. For there is no holiness where I am not.

30. Fear not when I fall in the fury of the storm; for mine acorns are blown afar by the wind; and verily I shall rise again, and my children about me, so that we shall uplift our forest in Eternity.

31. Eternity is the storm that covereth me.

32. I am Existence, the Existence that existeth not save through its own Existence, that is beyond the Existence of Existences, and rooted deeper than the No-Thing-Tree in the Land of No-Thing.

33. Now therefore thou knowest when I am within thee, when my hood is spread over thy skull, when my might is more than the penned Indus, and resistless as the Giant Glacier.

34. For as thou art before a lewd woman in Thy nakedness in the bazar, sucked up by her slyness and smiles, so art thou wholly and no more in part before the symbol of the beloved, though it be but a Pisacha or a Yantra or a Deva.

35. And in all shalt thou create the Infinite Bliss, and the next link of the Infinite Chain.

36. This chain reaches from Eternity to Eternity, ever in triangles—is not my symbol a triangle?—ever in

circles—is not the symbol of the Beloved a circle? Therein is all progress base illusion, for every circle is alike and every triangle alike!

37. But the progress is progress, and progress is rapture, constant, dazzling, showers of light, waves of dew, flames of the hair of the Great Goddess, flowers of the roses that are about her neck, Amen!

38. Therefore lift up thyself as I am lifted up. Hold thyself in as I am master to accomplish. At the end, be the end far distant as the stars that lie in the navel of Nuit, do thou slay thyself as I at the end am slain, in the death that is life, in the peace that is mother of war, in the darkness that holds light in his hand as a harlot that plucks a jewel from her nostrils.

39. So therefore the beginning is delight, and the End is delight, and delight is in the midst, even as the Indus is water in the cavern of the glacier, and water among the greater hills and the lesser hills and through the ramparts of the hills and through the plains, and water at the mouth thereof when it leaps forth into the mighty sea, yea, into the mighty sea.

# LIBER TAU vel

## KABBALÆ TRIUM LITERARUM

### SUB FIGURÂ

# CD

A∴A∴
Publication in Class A.

The Magister Templi, the Adeptus, the Neophyte [8° = 3°, 5° = 6°, 0° = 0°].

The Ultimate Illusion, the Illusion of Force, the Illusion of Matter.

The Functions of the 3 Orders: Silence in Speech; Silence; Speech in Silence: Construction, Preservation, Destruction.

The Supreme Unveiling (or Unveiling of Light), the Unveiling of Life, the Unveiling of Love.

Equilibrium; on the Cubic Stone, on the Path, and among the Shells.

The Rituals of Initiation, 8° = 3°, 5° = 6°, 0° = 0°: Asar, as Bull, as Man, as Sun.

The Ordeals of Initiation, 8° = 3°, 5° = 6°, 0° = 0°: Birth, Death, Resurrection.

LIBER

DCCCXIII

VEL

ARARITA

SUB FIGURÂ

DLXX

A∴A∴
Publication in Class A.

# I

## א

فل هو اللة احد اللة الصمد لم يلد ولم يولد ولم يكن له كفوا احد

0. O my God!  One is Thy Beginning!  One is Thy Spirit, and Thy Permutation One!
1. Let me extol Thy perfections before men.
2. In the Image of a Sixfold Star that flameth across the Vault inane, let me re-veil Thy perfections.
3. Thou hast appeared unto me as an agèd God, a venerable God, the Lord of Time, bearing a sharp sickle.
4. Thou hast appeared unto me as a jocund and ruddy God, full of Majesty, a King, a Father in his prime. Thou didst bear the sceptre of the Universe, crowned with the Wheel of the Spirit.
5. Thou hast appeared unto me with sword and spear, a warrior God in flaming armour among Thine horsemen.
6. Thou hast appeared unto me as a young and brilliant God, a god of music and beauty, even as a young god in his strength, playing upon the lyre.
7. Thou hast appeared unto me as the white foam of Ocean gathered into limbs whiter than the foam, the limbs of a

miracle of women, as a goddess of extreme love, bearing the girdle of gold.

8. Thou hast appeared to me as a young boy mischievous and lovely, with Thy winged globe and its serpents set upon a staff.

9. Thou hast appeared to me as an huntress among Thy dogs, as a goddess virginal chaste, as a moon among the faded oaks of the wood of years.

10. But I was deceived by none of these. All these I cast aside, crying: Begone! So that all these faded from my vision.

11. Also I welded together the Flaming Star and the Sixfold Star in the forge of my soul, and behold! a new star 418 that is above all these.

12. Yet even so was I not deceived; for the crown hath twelve rays.

13. And these twelve rays are one.

# II

ר

0. Now then I saw these things averse and evil; and they were not, even as Thou art Not.
1. I saw the twin heads that ever battle against one another, so that all their thought is a confusion. I saw Thee in these.
2. I saw the darkeners of wisdom, like black apes chattering vile nonsense. I saw Thee in these.
3. I saw the devouring mothers of Hell, that eat up their children—O ye that are without understanding! I saw Thee in these.
4. I saw the merciless and the unmajestic like harpies tearing their foul food. I saw Thee in these.
5. I saw the burning ones, giants like volcanoes belching out the black vomit of fire and smoke in their fury. I saw Thee in these.
6. I saw the petty, the quarrelsome, the selfish,—they were like men, O Lord, they were even like unto men. I saw Thee in these.
7. I saw the ravens of death, that flew with hoarse cries upon the carrion earth. I saw Thee in these.
8. I saw the lying spirits like frogs upon the earth, and upon the water, and upon the treacherous metal that corrodeth all things and abideth not. I saw Thee in these.

9. I saw the obscene ones, bull-men linked in the abyss of putrefaction, that gnawed each other's tongues for pain. I saw Thee in these.

10. I saw the Woman. O my God, I beheld the image thereof, even as a lovely shape that concealeth a black monkey, even as a figure that draweth with her hands small images of men down into hell. I saw her from the head to the navel a woman, from the navel to the feet of her a man. I saw Thee even in her.

11. For mine was the keyword to the Closed Palace 418 and mine the reins of the Chariot of the Sphinxes, black and white.

    But I was not deceived by anything of all these things.

12. For I expanded it by my subtlety into Twelve Rays of the Crown.

13. And these twelve rays were One.

# III

## א

0. Say thou that He God is one; God is the Everlasting One; nor hath He any Equal, or any Son, or any Companion. Nothing shall stand before His face.
1. Even for five hundred and eleven times nightly for one and forty days did I cry aloud unto the Lord the affirmation of His Unity.
2. Also did I glorify His wisdom, whereby He made the worlds.
3. Yea, I praised Him for His intelligible essence, whereby the universe became light.
4. I did thank Him for His manifold mercy; I did worship His magnificence and majesty.
5. I trembled before His might.
6. I delighted in the Harmony and Beauty of His Essence.
7. In His Victory I pursued His enemies; yea I drave them down the steep; I thundered after them into the utmost abyss; yea, therein I partook of the glory of my Lord.
8. His Splendour shone upon me; I adored His adorable splendour.
9. I rested myself, admiring the Stability of Him, how the shaking of His Universe, the dissolution of all things, should move Him not.
10. Yea, verily, I the Lord Viceregent of His Kingdom, I, Adonai, who speak unto my servant V.V.V.V.V. did rule and govern in His place.

11. Yet also did I formulate the word of double power in the Voice of the Master, even the word 418.

12. And all these things deceived me not, for I expanded them by my subtlety into the Twelve Rays of the Crown.

13. And these twelve rays were One.

# IV

ד

0. Also the little child, the lover of Adonai, even V.V.V.V.V., reflecting the glory of Adonai, lifted up his voice and said:

1. Glory to God, and Thanksgiving to God! There is One God alone, and God is exceeding great. He is about us, and there is no strength save in Him the exalted, the great.

2. Thus did V.V.V.V.V. become mad, and wend about naked.

3. And all these things fled away, for he understood them all, that they were but as old rags upon the Divine Perfection.

4. Also he pitied them all, that they were but reflections distorted.

5. Also he smote them, lest they should bear rule over the just.

6. Also he harmonized them into one picture, beautiful to behold.

7. And having thus conquered them, there was a certain glamour of holiness even in the hollow sphere of outward brilliance.

8. So that all became splendid.

9. And having firmly stablished them in order and disposition,

10. He proclaimed the perfection, the bride, the delight of God in His creation.

11. But though thus he worked, he tried ever his work by the Star 418.

12. And it deceived him not; for by his subtlety he expanded it all into the Twelve Rays of the Crown.

13. And these twelve rays were One.

# V

ק

0. In the place of the cross the indivisible point which hath no points nor parts nor magnitude. Nor indeed hath it position, being beyond space. Nor hath it existence in time, for it is beyond Time. Nor hath it cause or effect, seeing that its Universe is infinite every way, and partaketh not of these our conceptions.
1. So wrote οὐ μή the Exempt Adept, and the laughter of the Masters of the Temple abashed him not.
2. Nor was he ashamed, hearing the laughter of the little dogs of hell.
3. For he abode in his place, and his falsehood was truth in his place.
4. The little dogs cannot correct him, for they can do naught but bark.
5. The masters cannot correct him, for they say: Come and see.
6. And I came and saw, even I, Perdurabo, the Philosophus of the Outer College.
7. Yea, even I the man beheld this wonder.
8. And I could not deliver it unto myself.
9. That which established me is invisible and unknowable in its essence.
10. Only they who know IT may be known.
11. For they have the genius of the mighty sword 418.

12. And they are not deceived by any of these things; for by
their subtlety do they expand them all into the Twelve
Rays of the Crown.

13. And these twelve rays are One.

# VI

ה

0. Deeper and deeper into the mire of things!
    Farther and farther into the never-ending Expansion of
    the Abyss.
1. The great goddess that bendeth over the Universe is my
    mistress; I am the winged globe at her heart.
2. I contract ever as she ever expandeth;
3. At the end it is all one.
4. Our loves have brought to birth the Father and Creator of
    all things.
5. He hath established the elements; the æther, the air, the
    water, the earth, and the fire.
6. He hath established the wandering stars in their courses.
7. He hath ploughed with the seven stars of his Plough, that
    the Seven might move indeed, yet ever point to the un-
    changing One.
8. He hath established the Eight Belts, wherewith he hath
    girdled the globes.
9. He hath established the Trinity of Triads in all things,
    forcing fire into fire, and ordering all things in the Stable
    Abode of the Kings of Ægypt.
10. He hath established His rule in His kingdom.
11. Yet the Father also boweth unto the Power of the Star 418
    and thereby
12. In his subtlety He expandeth it all into twelve rays of the
    Crown.
13. And these twelve rays are One.

# VII

א

0. Then in the might of the Lion did I formulate unto myself that holy and formless fire, קדש, which darteth and flasheth through the depths of the Universe.
1. At the touch of the Fire Qadosh the earth melted into a liquor clear as water.
2. At the touch of the Fire Qadosh the water smoked into a lucid air.
3. At the touch of the Fire Qadosh the air ignited, and became Fire.
4. At the touch of the Fire Qadosh, O Lord, the Fire dissipated into Space.
5. At the touch of the Fire Qadosh, O Lord, the Space resolved itself into a Profundity of Mind.
6. At the touch of the Fire Qadosh the Mind of the Father was broken up into the brilliance of our Lord the Sun.
7. At the touch of the Fire Qadosh the Brilliance of our Lord was absorbed in the Naught of our Lady of the Body of the Milk of the Stars.
8. Then only was the Fire Qadosh extinguished, when the Enterer was driven back from the threshold,
9. And the Lord of Silence was established upon the Lotus flower.
10. Then was accomplished all that which was to be accomplished.

11. And All and One and Naught were slain in the slaying of the Warrior 418,

12. In the slaying of the subtlety that expanded all these things into the Twelve Rays of the Crown,

13. That returned unto One, and beyond One, even unto the vision of the Fool in his folly that chanted the word Ararita, and beyond the Word and the Fool; yea, beyond the Word and the Fool.

# APPENDICES

# APPENDIX A
## The Stèle of Revealing

This appendix is comprised of reference material for the study of the Stèle (or Stela)* of Revealing. It includes « The Stèle, Translation and Other Matters Pertaining to Liber Legis, » an hitherto-unpublished document that figured prominently in the circumstances surrounding the reception of *Liber Legis*, as recounted above (Preface, pp. xi–xii). This document was produced by the Boulaq Museum in Cairo, where the Stèle bore the catalogue number 666. As adjuncts to this document, pertinent materials from Crowley's published works have been collected for republication. Finally, a modern, analytical translation of the Stèle has been prepared for this edition. In all, three separate translations are included, each characteristic of an important school of Egyptian lexicography. Photographs of the Stèle are also included, reproduced opposite transcriptions of the hieroglyphic texts.

The following synopsis lists the contents of this appendix with an explanation of the editorial treatment given each section.

A. *The Stèle, Translation and Other Matters Pertaining to Liber Legis.*

This document was given its title by Aleister Crowley, and survives in holograph manuscript. Prepared in 1904 E.V., it is contemporary with *Liber Legis*, and includes the translation prepared for Crowley by the assistant curator of the Boulaq Museum in Cairo, under the supervision of the Egyptologist Brugsch Bey. It can be conveniently subdivided into five sections:

1. Rough sketches of the obverse and reverse of the Stèle, replaced in this appendix by photographs, at 31% of the Stèle's actual dimensions of 51.5 × 31 cm.

---

* A note on the orthography of the word *stèle* is necessary here. Crowley's writings, beginning with *Liber Legis*, give the word as « stélé, » whereas correct usage is either *stèle* or *stela*, one derived from Latin, the other from Greek. No attempt to « correct » *Liber Legis* has been considered, but elsewhere in the present volume the usage is *stèle*, taking precedent from « La Traduction du Musée Boulaq. »

2. A transcription, or fair copy, of the Egyptian hieroglyphic texts. These have been recopied for publication, and are reproduced opposite the photographs of the Stèle as an aid to study.

3. A tabular, word-by-word analysis of each Egyptian text, giving the roman transliteration and a French translation. Originally entitled «Stèle 666,» an editorial subtitle has been given to this section, «L'Analyse du Musée Boulaq» («The Boulaq Museum Analysis»). It is reproduced verbatim, with the editorial addition of a modern English translation of the original French in a fourth tabular column. The hieroglyphs were recopied for publication.

4. A French prose translation (with a descriptive commentary) that differs in certain details from «L'Analyse du Musée Boulaq,» and probably represents the Boulaq Museum translator's final draft. Also originally entitled «Stèle 666,» this section has been given the editorial subtitle «La Traduction du Musée Boulaq,» and is reproduced verbatim. A modern English translation of the French, entitled «Stèle 666: The Boulaq Museum Translation,» has been supplied for publication.

5. A colophon note of acknowledgement by Crowley, reproduced verbatim between the original French of «Stèle 666: La Traduction du Musée Boulaq» and its English translation.

B. *A Paraphrase of the Stèle of Revealing.*

Just prior to the reception of *Liber Legis* in 1904 E.V., Crowley prepared an English versification of the principal texts of the Stèle, based upon the Boulaq Museum translation, parts of which are incorporated into *Liber Legis*. This poetic paraphrase, first published in 1912 E.V., was later reissued in *The Equinox of the Gods*, from which it is republished.* The title, «A Paraphrase of the Stèle of Revealing,» is an editorial distillation of the two longer titles given by Crowley.

C. *Stèle of Ankh-f-na-Khonsu: The Gardiner-Gunn Translation.*

During the period 1904–12 E.V. Crowley commissioned another translation of the Stèle from two prominent British Egyptologists, Sir Alan Gardiner and Battiscombe Gunn. Like the «Paraphrase,» this translation first appeared in 1912 E.V. and was reissued (with

---

* *See* J.F.C. Fuller, «The Temple of Solomon the King,» *The Equinox* I(7) (London, 1912) and Crowley, *The Equinox of the Gods* (London: O.T.O., 1936). In the «Paraphrase,» Crowley's use of the word «Duant» for the Egyptian *Duaut* (or *Duat*) probably owes to a misreading of the MS. of «La Traduction du Musée Boulaq,» where the *u* is easily confused with an *n*. The word «Duant» occurs in the Holy Books, and is retained as such. In the «Paraphrase,» however, it has been corrected to read *Duaut*.

variations) in *The Equinox of the Gods*, from which it is republished. The footnotes to this translation are original. However, an editorial subtitle, « The Gardiner-Gunn Translation,» has been supplied to minimize confusion with other translations in this appendix.

D. *A Modern Analysis.*

A new analytical translation is included that was prepared in 1982 E.V. for inclusion in this appendix. This translation reflects the advances in Egyptian lexicography achieved in the past seventy years, and employs the Egyptian transliteration generally used in modern reference works. To facilitate comparison, its tabular format emulates that of the Boulaq Museum analysis.

In order to facilitate cross-reference between the translations and the transcriptions of the Egyptian hieroglyphs, the six segments of the Stèle have been indexed from A to F, with line numbers provided wherever necessary. Such editorial additions appear enclosed in brackets.

Finally, owing to the many separate documents reproduced, a table of contents to the appendix is provided below.

# TABLE OF CONTENTS
## APPENDIX A

[A]

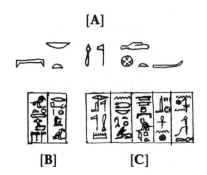

[B]     [C]

[D]

[E]

## Reverse

**[F]**

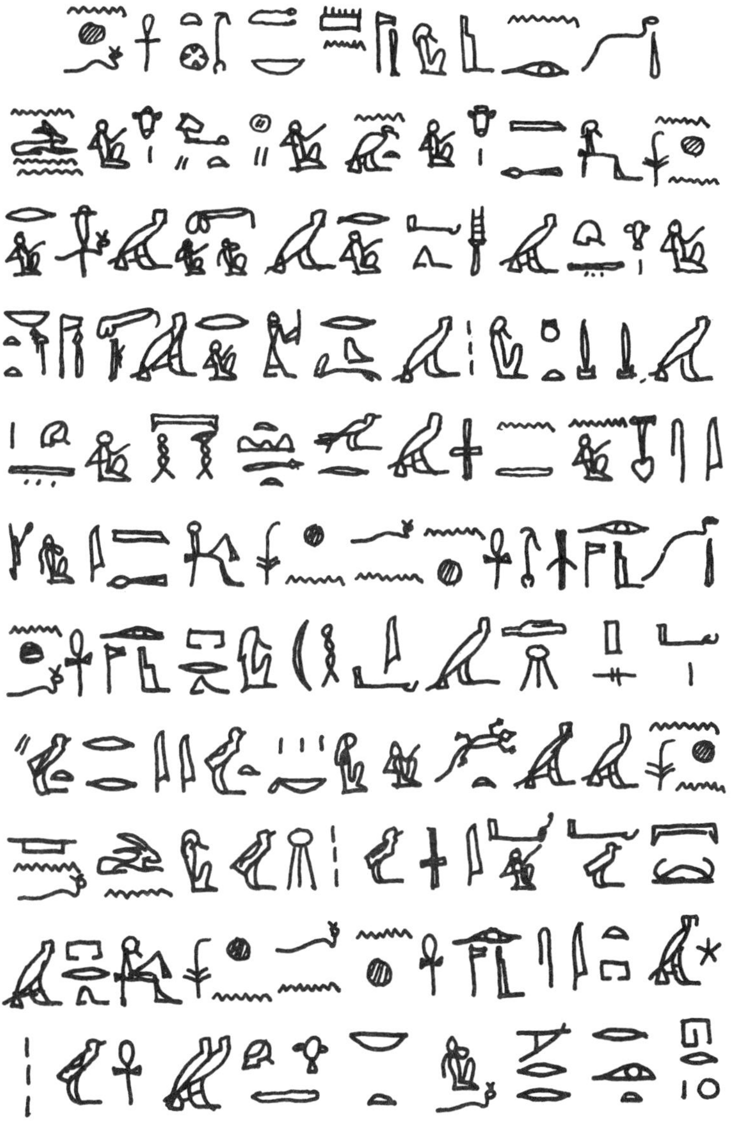

# STÈLE 666
## [L'ANALYSE DU MUSÉE BOULAQ/
## THE BOULAQ MUSEUM ANALYSIS]
### [FACE PRINCIPALE/OBVERSE]

**[A]**

|  |  | *Sous le disque ailé:* | *Under the winged disk:* |
|---|---|---|---|
|  | *Hud·t* | Hudit | Hudit |
|  | *nuter* | dieu | god |
|  | *ââ* | grand | great |
|  | *neb* | Seigneur | Lord |
|  | *t* | le | the |
|  | *pet* | ciel | sky |

**[B]**

|  |  | *Sur le dieu:* | *Above the god:* |
|---|---|---|---|
|  | *Râ* | Râ | Ra |
|  | *Hor* | ⎰Hor | ⎰Hor |
|  | *Khut* | ⎱khut | ⎱khut |
|  | *her* | chef | chief |
|  | *nuteru* | dieux | gods |

**[C]**

|  |  | *Sur l'adorant:* | *Above the worshipper:* |
|---|---|---|---|
|  | *As·ar* | Osiris (le défunt) | Osiris (the deceased) |
|  | *nuter hon* | esclave de dieu (prophète) | slave of god (prophet) |
|  | *Ment* | Mentu | Mentu |
|  | *neb* | Seigneur | Lord |
|  | *was·t* | Thèbes | Thebes |
|  | *un* | ouvrant | opening |
|  | *ââu* | les portes | the doors |
|  | *nu* | du | of |
|  | *pet* | ciel | sky |
|  | *m* | dans | in |

| | | | |
|---|---|---|---|
| 𓃾𓏏𓅱 | *apetu* | Thèbes (Karnak) | Thebes (Karnak) |
| 𓋹𓆑 | *ankh f* | ⎧ Ank·f   Il vit | ⎧ Ank·f   He lives |
| 𓆖𓐍𓈖𓋴𓅱 | *n khonsu* | ⎩ n khonsu   par Khonsu | ⎩ n khonsu   in Khonsu |

**[D]**        [*no translation*]

**[E]**

| | | | | |
|---|---|---|---|---|
| [1] | 𓂧𓂧 | *Zod* | Dit | Said |
| | 𓈖 | *n* | par | by |
| | 𓁹𓊨 | *asar* | défunt | the deceased |
| | 𓊹 | *nuter hon* | prophète | prophet |
| | 𓏴 | *ment* | Menthou | Menthou |
| | 𓎟 | *neb* | Seigneur | Lord |
| | 𓏏 | *t* | de la | of the |
| | 𓊖 | *uas-t* | Thèbaide | Thebaid |
| | 𓏏𓈖𓏌 | *un* | ouvrant | opening |
| | 𓂣𓂣 | *āāu* | les portes | the doors |
| | 𓈗 | *nu* | de | of |
| | 𓏏 | *t* | le | the |
| | 𓇯 | *pet* | ciel | sky |
| | 𓅓 | *m* | dans | in |
| | 𓃾𓏏𓅱 | *aptu* | Thèbes | Thebes |
| [1–2] | 𓋹𓆑𓈖𓊾 | *ānkh f n khonsu* | Ankh f n khonsu | Ankh f n khonsu |
| | 𓐍𓂋𓅱 | *mâ kheru* | vrai de voix | true-of-voice |
| | 𓀠 | *a* | Ô | O |
| | 𓂝𓀠 | *ka* | élevé, sublime | elevated, sublime |
| | 𓀢 | *dua* | adore | adore |
| | 𓀯 | *tuf* | lui | him |
| | 𓄂 | *ur* | grandeur | greatness |
| | 𓃝 | *biu* | des Esprits, | of Spirits, |
| | 𓀾 | *bi* | esprit | spirit |
| | 𓂝𓂝 | *āā* | grand | great |

| | | | |
|---|---|---|---|
| | *chefu* | des craintes | of fears, |
| | *dudu* | donnant | giving |
| | *ner f* | terreur de lui | the terror of him |
| [3] | *n* | aux | to |
| | *neteru* | dieux | the gods |
| | *khâ* | élevé, apparaissant | elevated, appearing |
| | *her* | sur | upon |
| | *nest* | trône | throne |
| | *f* | de lui | of his |
| | *ur* | grand | great |
| | *ar* | faisant | making |
| | *watu* | les voies | the ways |
| | *n* | à | to |
| | *bi* | l'esprit | the spirit |
| | *n khu* | au lumineuse | to the bright one |
| | *n khab* | à l'ombre, au corps | to the shadow, to the body |
| | *au* | étant | being |
| | *aper* | muni | provided |
| | *ku* | moi | I |
| | *khu* | lumineuse | bright one |
| [4] | *am* | là | there |
| | *aper* | muni | provided |
| | *ar n a* | j'ai fait | I have made |
| | *uat* | chemin | road |
| | *r* | vers | towards |
| | *but* | le lieu | the place |
| | *nti* | où est | where is |
| | *rā* | Râ | Ra |
| | *tum* | Tum | Tum |
| | *khepra* | Khepra | Khepra |
| | *hathor* | Hathor | Hathor |

| | Transliteration | French | English |
|---|---|---|---|
| | am | là. | there. |
| | asar | défunt | deceased |
| | hon | prophète | prophet |
| | ment neb uas | de Mentu seigneur de Thèbes | of Mentu lord of Thebes |
| [5] | ankh f n khonsu | Ankh f n khonsu | Ankh f n khonsu |
| | si | fils | son |
| | ma nen | du semblable | of the equivalent |
| | bi sa | ⎧ Bes | ⎧ Bes |
| | n mut | ⎩ n mut; | ⎩ n mut; |
| | ar n | fils de | son of |
| | ahit | la prêtresse-musicienne | the priestess-musician |
| | n amen râ | d'Ammon râ | of Amun-re |
| | neb pa | maîtresse de la maison | mistress of the house |
| | ta | ⎧ Ta | ⎧ Ta |
| | nech | ⎩ nech | ⎩ nech |

[REVERS/REVERSE]

**[F]**

| | Transliteration | French | English |
|---|---|---|---|
| [1] | zed | Dit | Said |
| | n | par | by |
| | asar | le défunt | the deceased |
| | nuter hon | prophète | prophet |
| | ment | de Mentu | of Mentu |
| | neb | seigneur | lord |
| | uast | de Thèbes | of Thebes |
| [1–2] | ānkh f n khonsu | Ankh f n Khonsu | Ankh f n Khonsu |
| | mā kheru | vrai de voix | true-of-voice |
| | hāti a | Mon cœur | My heart |
| | n | de | of |
| | mut a | ma mère | my mother |
| | sep sen | (bis) | (twice) |

| | Transliteration | French | English |
|---|---|---|---|
| | *hati a* | mon cœur | my heart |
| | *n* | de | of |
| | *unn a* | mon existence | my existence |
| [3] | *her tep to* | sur terre, | on earth, |
| | *m* | ne pas | do not |
| | *hā* | dresse | stand up |
| | *r a* | contre moi | against me |
| | *m* | comme | as |
| | *met a* | mon accusateur, | my accuser, |
| | *m* | ne pas | do not |
| | *khesef* | pousse | press |
| | *r a* | contre moi | against me |
| [4] | *m* | parmi | among |
| | *zazanetu* | les juges, | the judges, |
| | *m* | ne pas | do not |
| | *rek* | fais opposition | make opposition |
| | *r a* | contre moi | against me |
| | *m bah* | devant | before |
| | *nuter âā* | le dieu grand | the great god |
| | *neb* | seigneur | lord |
| | *amenti* | de l'Occident | of the West; |
| [5] | *as* | car | because |
| | *sam* | réuni | united |
| | *n a* | j'ai | I have |
| | *to pet* | la terre, le ciel | the land, the sky |
| | *am urt* | l'Ouest | the West |
| | *aat* | le grand | the great |
| | *pet* | du ciel, | of the sky, |
| | *uah a* | je florissais | I have flourished |
| | *tep to* | sur terre. | on earth. |
| [6] | *Zed* | Dit | Said |
| | *asar* | le défunt | the deceased |
| | *...uas* | prêtre thèbain | Theban priest |

| | ānkh f n knonsu | Ankh f n khonsu | Ankh f n khonsu |
|---|---|---|---|
| | mā kheru | vrai de voix | true-of-voice |
| | a | Ô! | O |
| [6–7] | uā dod | un bras | an arm |
| | pesd | brilliant | shining |
| | m | dans | in |
| | aāh | la lune, | the moon |
| | per | sort | goes forth |
| | asar | le défunt | the deceased |
| [7–8] | ankh f n khonsu | Ankh-f-n-khonsu | Ankh-f-n-khonsu |
| | ami achtu | parmi les multitudes | among the multitudes |
| | ketiu | franchissant | passing through |
| [8–9] | reruti | les portes | the doors |
| | uhāu a | je rejoins | I gather together |
| | amu | (ceux qui sont) parmis | (those who are) among |
| | khu | la clarté | the brightness |
| | un n f | il a ouvert | he has opened |
| [10] | duat | le Duaut (région des étoiles); | the Duaut (the region of the stars); |
| | as | alors | now then |
| | asar | le défunt | the deceased |
| | ankh f n khonsu | Ankh f n khonsu | Ankh f n khonsu |
| | per | sort | goes forth |
| | m | du | by |
| [11] | her | jour | day |
| | r | pour | to |
| | art | faire | do |
| | merer f | ses volontés | his wishes |
| | nebet | toutes | all |
| | her tep to | de sur terre | of what is on earth |
| | ami | parmi | among |
| | ankhu | les vivants | the living |

# STÈLE 666
## [LA TRADUCTION DU MUSÉE BOULAQ]

*Stèle en bois stuqué[e] et peinte, à double face[s], cintrée au sommet,
portant le n° 666 au catalogue.*

### FACE PRINCIPALE

[A] Le tableau du haut est encadré par une représentation de la déesse
du ciel, Nout, dont le corps est allongé, et les bras pendant de telle
sorte que le bout des doigts touche le sol. Au dessous est le disque
ailé du soleil avec son nom «*Houdit*, dieu grand, seigneur du ciel».

[B–C] Le tableau montre un prêtre revêtu de la peau de panthère
debout devant le dieu Harmakhis assis sur son trône, derrière
lequel est l'emblême de l'Occident. La légende du dieu est
«Ra-Hor-khut, chef des dieux»; celle de l'adorant «Le défunt,
prophète de Mentou, seigneur de Thèbes, à qui sont ouvertes les
portes du ciel dans Thèbes, *Ankh-f-n-khonsu*».

[D] Devant le prêtre est une table d'offrandes sous laquelle est inscrit
«pains, eau, bœufs, oies».

[E] Le texte du bas se traduit: «Le défunt, prophète de Mentou,
seigneur de Thèbes, à qui sont ouvertes les portes du ciel dans
Thèbes, *Ankh-f-n-khonsu*, à la voix juste, dit: ‹O sublime! j'adore la
grandeur de tes esprits, âme très redoutable, qui inspire sa terreur
aux dieux. Apparaissant sur son grand trône, il fait les voies de
l'âme, de l'esprit et du corps ayant reçu la lumière en étant muni[s],
j'ai fait ma route vers l'endroit où sont Râ, Toum, Khepra et
Hathor, moi, le défunt prophète de Mentou, seigneur de Thèbes,
*Ankh-f-n-khonsu*, fils du personnage de même rang, *Bes-n-maut* et de
la prêtresse d'Ammon-râ, la maîtresse de maison *Ta-nech*».

### REVERS

[F] Inscription en bleu foncé sur fond blanc: «Le défunt, prophéte de
Mentou, seigneur de Thèbes, Ankh-f-n-khonsu, à la voix juste, dit:
‹O mon cœur, de ma mère, le cœur que j'avais sur terre, ne te
dresse pas contre moi en témoin, ne t'oppose pas à moi comme
juge, ne me charge pas en présence du dieu grand, seigneur de
l'Occident, car j'ai rejoint la terre au grand Occident quand j'étais
florissant sur terre!› Le défunt prêtre de Thèbes, *Ankh-f-n-khonsu* à

la voix juste, dit: ‹Ô, celui qui n'a qu'un bras, qui brille dans la lune, le défunt *Ankh-f-n-khonsu* a quitté les multitudes et rejoint ceux qui sont dans la lumière, il a ouvert la demeure des étoiles (le Duaut); alors le défunt *Ankh-f-n-khonsu* est sorti[r] du jour pour faire tout ce qui lui plaisait sur terre, parmi[s] les vivants.› »

Provient de Gournah (Thèbes) XXVIᵉ dynastie.

### [ACKNOWLEDGEMENT]

We are indebted to the kindness of Brugsch Bey & M. [. . .] for the above translation of the stèle whose discovery led to the creation of the ritual by which Aiwass, the author of *Liber L* [*Liber AL*], was invoked.

[— *Aleister and Rose Crowley*]


# STÈLE 666
## [THE BOULAQ MUSEUM TRANSLATION]

*Wooden stèle overlain with stucco and painted, double-sided, rounded at the top, bearing the number 666 in the catalogue.*

### OBVERSE

[A] The upper scene is framed by a representation of the goddess of the sky, Nout, whose body is elongated and whose arms are hanging down in such a manner that her fingertips touch the ground. Below is the winged disk of the sun with its name «*Houdit*, the great god, lord of the sky.»

[B–C] The scene shows a priest dressed in a panther skin standing before the god Harmakhis who is seated on his throne, beyond which there is the insignia of the West. The caption for the god reads: «Ra-Hor-khut, chief of the gods»; that of the worshipper reads: «The deceased, prophet of Mentou, lord of Thebes, the one for whom the doors of the sky are opened in Thebes, *Ankh-f-n-khonsu.*»

[D] In front of the priest is a table of offerings under which is written «bread, water, cattle and fowl.»

[E]  The lower text is translated as follows: « The deceased, the prophet of Mentou, lord of Thebes, *Ankh-f-n-khonsu*, true-of-voice, says: ‹ O sublime one! I adore the greatness of your spirits, o formidable soul, who inspires terror of himself among the gods. Appearing on his great throne, he travels the path of the soul, of the spirit, and of the body, having received the light, being equipped, I have made my path towards the place in which Ra, Toum, Khepra and Hathor are; I, the deceased priest of Mentou, lord of Thebes, *Ankh-f-n-khonsu*, son of a person of the same rank, *Bes-n-maut*, and of the priestess of Ammon-ra, the mistress of the house *Ta-nech*.› »

## REVERSE

[F]  Inscription in blue sunk into a white background: « The deceased, prophet of Mentou, lord of Thebes, Ankh-f-n-khonsu, true-of-voice, says: ‹O my heart of my mother, O heart which I had while I was on earth, do not rise up against me in witness, do not oppose me as a judge, do not charge me in the presence of the great god, lord of the West, because I have joined the land to the great West when I was flourishing on earth!› The deceased, priest of Thebes, *Ankh-f-n-khonsu*, true-of-voice, says: ‹O, you who only has one arm, who shines in the moon, the deceased *Ankh-f-n-khonsu* has left the multitudes and rejoined those who are in the light, he has opened the dwelling-place of the stars (the Duaut); now then, the deceased *Ankh-f-n-khonsu* has gone forth by day in order to do everything that pleased him upon earth, among the living.› »

Provenance — Gurna (Thebes) XXVI[TH] Dynasty.

# [A PARAPHRASE OF THE STÈLE OF REVEALING]

## A PARAPHRASE OF THE INSCRIPTIONS UPON THE OBVERSE OF THE STÈLE OF REVEALING

Above, the gemmèd azure is
    The naked splendour of Nuit;
She bends in ecstasy to kiss
    The secret ardours of Hadit.
The wingèd globe, the starry blue
Are mine, o Ankh-f-n-Khonsu.


I am the Lord of Thebes, and I
    The inspired forth-speaker of Mentu;
For me unveils the veilèd sky,
    The self-slain Ankh-f-n-Khonsu
Whose words are truth.  I invoke, I greet
Thy presence, o Ra-Hoor-Khuit!


Unity uttermost showed!
    I adore the might of Thy breath,
Supreme and terrible God,
    Who makest the gods and death
        To tremble before Thee: —
        I, I adore thee!


Appear on the throne of Ra!
    Open the ways of the Khu!
Lighten the ways of the Ka!
    The ways of the Khabs run through
        To stir me or still me!
        Aum! let it fill me!

The Light is mine; its rays consume
    Me: I have made a secret door
Into the House of Ra and Tum,
    Of Khephra, and of Ahathoor.
I am thy Theban, o Mentu,
The prophet Ankh-f-n-Khonsu!


By Bes-na-Maut my breast I beat;
    By wise Ta-Nech I weave my spell.
Show thy star-splendour, O Nuith!
    Bid me within thine House to dwell,
O wingèd snake of light, Hadith!
Abide with me, Ra-Hoor-Khuit!

A PARAPHRASE OF THE HIEROGLYPHS OF THE
11 LINES UPON THE REVERSE OF THE STÈLE

Saith of Mentu the truth-telling brother
    Who was master of Thebes from his birth:
O heart of me, heart of my mother!
    O heart which I had upon earth!
Stand not thou up against me a witness!
    Oppose me not, judge, in my quest!
Accuse me not now of unfitness
    Before the Great God, the dread Lord of the West!
For I fastened the one to the other
    With a spell for their mystical girth,
The earth and the wonderful West,
    When I flourished, o earth, on thy breast!

The dead man Ankh-f-n-Khonsu
    Saith with his voice of truth and calm:
O thou that hast a single arm!
    O thou that glitterest in the moon!
I weave thee in the spinning charm;
    I lure thee with the billowy tune.

The dead man Ankh-f-n-Khonsu
    Hath parted from the darkling crowds,
Hath joined the dwellers of the light,
    Opening Duaut, the star-abodes,
    Their keys receiving.
The dead man Ankh-f-n-Khonsu
    Hath made his passage into night,
His pleasure on the earth to do
    Among the living.

# STÈLE OF ANKH-F-NA-KHONSU
## [THE GARDINER–GUNN TRANSLATION]

### OBVERSE

[A] *Topmost Register (under Winged Disk).*
Behdet (? Hadit?), the Great God, the Lord of Heaven.

*Middle Register.*
[B]    *Two vertical lines to left:* —
Ra-Harakhti, Master of the Gods.

[C]    *Five vertical lines to right:* —
Osiris, the Priest of Montu, Lord of Thebes, Opener of the
doors of Nut in Karnak, Ankh-f-n-Khonsu, the Justified.

[D] *Below Altar:* —
Oxen, Geese, Wine (?), Bread.
> *Behind the god is the hieroglyph of Amenti.*

[E] *Lowest Register.*
(1) Saith Osiris, the Priest of Montu, Lord of Thebes, the Opener of
the Doors of Nut in Karnak, Ankh-f-n-Khonsu, (2) the Justified: —
«Hail, Thou whose praise is high (the highly praised), thou
great-willed. O Soul (*ba*) very awful (*lit.* mighty, of awe) that giveth
the terror of him (3) among the Gods, shining in glory upon his
great throne, making ways for the Soul (*ba*) for the Spirit (*yekh*) and
for the Shadow (*khabt*): I am prepared and I shine forth as one that
is prepared. (4) I have made way to the place in which are Ra,
Tom, Khepri and Hathor.» Osiris, the Priest of Montu, Lord of
Thebes (5) Ankh-f-na-Khonsu, the Justified; son of MNBSNMT*;
born of the Sistrum-bearer of Amon, the Lady Atne-sher.

---

* The father's name. The method of spelling shows he was a foreigner. There is no
clue to the vocalization.

## REVERSE

**[F]**  *Eleven lines of writing.*

(1) Saith Osiris, the Priest of Montu, Lord of Thebes, Ankh-f-(2)na-khonsu, the Justified: «My heart from my mother, my heart from my mother, my heart* of my existence (3) upon earth, stand not forth against me as witness, drive me not back (4) among the Sovereign Judges,† neither incline against me in the presence of the Great God, the Lord of the West.‡ (5) Now that I am united with Earth in the Great West, and endure no longer upon Earth.»

(6) Saith Osiris, he who is in Thebes, Ankh-f-na-Khonsu, the Justified: «O Only (7) One, shining like (*or* in) the Moon; Osiris Ankh-f-(8)na-Khonsu has come forth upon high among these thy multitudes. (9) He that gathereth together those that are in the Light, the Underworld (*duat*) is (also) (10) opened to him; lo Osiris Ankh-f-na-Khonsu, cometh forth (11) by day to do all that he wisheth upon earth among the living.»

---

* Different word, apparently synonymous, but probably not so at all.
† Quite an arbitrary and conventional translation of the original word.
‡ Osiris, of course.

# A MODERN ANALYSIS

## OBVERSE

**[A]**

| | *bḥdt* | The Beḥedite |
| | *nṯr ꜥꜣ* | the great god |
| | *nb(t)* | Lord (of) |
| | *pt* | the sky |

**[B]**

| | *r ꜥ* | Re- |
| | *ḥr-ꜣḫty* | Horakhty |
| | *ḥry* | chieftain (of) |
| | *nṯrw* | the gods |

**[C]**

| | *wsir* | The Osiris |
| | *ḥm-nṯr* | the priest (of) |
| | *mnṯ(w)* | Monthu |
| | *nb* | Lord (of) |
| | *wꜣst* | Thebes |
| | *wn* | the opener (of) |
| | *ꜥꜣwy* | the doors |
| | *nw* | of |
| | *pt* | the sky |
| | *m* | in |
| | *ipt-swt* | Karnak |
| | *ꜥnḫif-n-ḫnsw* | Ankhef-n-Khonsu |
| | *[mꜣꜥ-]ḫrw (defectively)* | justified |

**[D]**

| | *t* | bread |
| | *ḥnkt* | beer |
| | *kꜣw ꜣpdw* | cattle and fowl |

**[E]**

| | | |
|---|---|---|
| [1] | *ḏd mdw (i)n* | Words spoken by |
| | *wsir* | the Osiris |
| | *ḥm-nṯr* | the priest |
| | *mnṯw* | of Monthu |
| | *nb(t)* | Lord (of) |
| | *wꜣst* | Thebes |
| | *wn* | the one who opens |
| | *ꜥꜣwy* | the doors |
| | *nw(t)* | of |
| | *pt* | the sky |
| | *m* | in |
| | *ipt-swt* | Karnak |
| [1–2] | *ꜥnḫ·f-n-ḫnsw* | Ankhef-en-Khonsu |
| | *mꜣꜥ-ḫrw* | justified |
| | *i* | O |
| | *kꜣ* | high one |
| | *dwꜣ·tw·f* | may he be praised |
| | *wr* | the one great of |
| | *bꜣw* | power |
| | *bꜣ* | the spirit |
| | *ꜥꜣ* | great of |
| | *šfyt* | dignity |
| | *ddw* | who places |
| | *nrw·f* | fear of himself |
| [3] | *n* | among (*lit:* to) |
| | *nṯrw* | the gods |
| | *ḥꜥw* | who shines forth |
| | *ḥr* | upon |
| | *nst·f* | his seat |
| | *wr* | great |
| | *ir* | make |

| | | |
|---|---|---|
| | *wȝwt* | way(s) |
| | *n* | for |
| | *bȝ(·i)* | (my) soul |
| | *n* | for |
| | *ȝḫ(·i)* | (my) spirit |
| | *n* | for |
| | *šw(t)(·i)* | (my) shadow |
| [4] | *iw* | (for) I |
| | *ꜥpr·kwi* | am equipped |
| | *wbn(·i)* | (so that) I might shine forth |
| | *im* | as |
| | *ꜥpr* | an equipped one |
| | *ir* | make |
| | *n·i* | for me |
| | *wȝt* | way |
| | *r* | to |
| | *bt* | the place |
| | *ntt* | which |
| | *rꜥ* | Ra |
| | *itm* | Atum |
| | *ḫpri* | Kheperi |
| | *ḥwt-ḥr* | Hathor |
| | *im* | (are) in |
| | *wsir ḥm-nṯr* | the Osiris, priest (of) |
| | *mnṯw* | Monthu |
| | *nb* | Lord (of) |
| | *wȝst* | Thebes |
| [5] | *ꜥnḫ·f-n-ḫnsw* | Ankhef-en-Khonsu |
| | *[mȝꜥ]-ḫrw* | justified (*written defectively*) |
| | *sȝ mi nw* | the son of a man with the same titles |
| | *bs-n-mwt* | Bes-en-mut |

| | *ir·n* | engendered of |
|---|---|---|
| | *iḥyt* | the musician |
| | *n* | of |
| | *imn-rˁ* | Amun-Re |
| | *nb(t)-pr* | the mistress of the house |
| | *t3-nši* | Taneshi |

## Reverse

### [F]

| | | | |
|---|---|---|---|
| [1] | | *ḏd mdw* | Words spoken |
| | | *(i)n* | by |
| | | *wsir* | the Osiris |
| | | *ḥm-nṯr* | the priest |
| | | *mnṯ(w)* | (of) Monthu |
| | | *nb* | Lord |
| | | *w3st* | of Thebes |
| | | *ˁnḫ·f-* | Ankh-ef- |
| [2] | | *n-ḫnsw* | -en-Khonsu |
| | | *m3ˁ-ḫrw* | justified. |
| | | *ib·i* | (O) my heart |
| | | *n* | of |
| | | *mwt·i* | my mother |
| | | *sp sn* | (two times) |
| | | *ḥ3ty·i* | (O) my heart |
| | | *n* | of |
| | | *wnn·i* | while I am |
| [3] | | *tp t3* | upon earth |
| | | *m* | do not |
| | | *ˁḥˁ* | rise up |
| | | *r·i* | against me |

| | | |
|---|---|---|
| | *m* | as |
| | *mty·i* | my witness |
| | *m* | do not |
| | *ḫsf* | oppose |
| | *r·i* | me |
| [4] | *m* | in |
| | *ḏ3ḏ3t* | the tribunal |
| | *m* | do not |
| | *rḳ* | be inimical |
| | *r·i* | against me |
| | *m-b3ḥ* | in the presence of |
| | *nṯr ʿ3* | the Great God |
| | *nb* | Lord (of) |
| | *imntt* | the West |
| [5] | *is* | although |
| | *sm3·n·i* | I have joined (myself) |
| | *n t3* | to the earth |
| | *imy-wrt* | in the western side |
| | *ʿ3t* | great |
| | *pt* | (of) the sky |
| | *w3ḥ·i* | may I endure |
| | *tp t3* | upon earth |
| [6] | *ḏd mdw (in)* | words spoken (by) |
| | *wsir* | the Osiris |
| | *sm3* | the *sm3*-priest |
| | *w3st* | (of Thebes) |
| | *ʿnḫ·f-n-ḫnsw* | Ankh-ef-en-Khonsu |
| | *m3ʿ-ḫrw* | justified |
| | *i* | O |
| [6–7] | *wʿw* | Unique One |
| | *psḏ* | who shines |
| | *m* | as |

| | | |
|---|---|---|
| | *iʿḥ* | the moon |
| | *pr* | may go forth |
| | *wsir* | the Osiris |
| | *ʿnḫ·f-* | Ankh-ef- |
| [8] | *-n-ḫnsw* | en-Khonsu |
| | *m-m* | among |
| | *ʿšɜw·k* | your multitude |
| | *twi* | this |
| | *r* | to |
| | *rwty* | the outside |
| [9] | *wḥʿ w* | (O) deliverer (of) |
| | *imyw* | (those) who are in |
| | *ɜḥw* | the sunshine |
| | *wn* | open |
| | *n·f* | for him |
| [10] | *dwɜt* | the netherworld |
| | *is* | indeed |
| | *wsir* | the Osiris |
| | *ʿnḫ·f-n-ḫnsw* | Ankh-ef-en-Khonsu |
| | *pr* | shall go forth |
| | *m* | by |
| [11] | *hrw* | day |
| | *r* | to |
| | *irt* | do |
| | *mrr(t)·f* | that which he desires |
| | *nbt* | all |
| | *tp tɜ* | upon earth |
| | *m-m* | among |
| | *ʿnḫw* | the living |

# APPENDIX B
## Technical Bibliography

This appendix is intended to afford an overview of Thelemic literature by providing a comprehensive reference list. It is organized serially, by the numbers assigned to the texts. Only the number, class and title of a particular text is listed — further reference to published sources would exceed the limited scope of this appendix. Since the latest known classification of a text is cited, it may be consulted to verify the class of a particular book or paper; several *libri* were reclassified by Crowley during his lifetime. This list may also prove useful in verifying the provenance of a particular work, since many apocryphal additions to the canon have appeared in recent years.

Scholastic questions concerning provenance, survival, classification, title or authorship are not specifically addressed in this booklist. Such questions should be researched, but the inclusion of preliminary results in a work of reference would later prove misleading. Accordingly, many open questions are retained in this list, *i.e.* books with two assigned numbers, alternate titles, *etc.* To facilitate research, an annotated version of this appendix, cross-referenced to published sources, is maintained and periodically reissued by O.T.O.

The vast majority of the papers listed are published, and most unpublished texts survive in manuscript; very few are believed lost. Most, but not all, of the papers were authored by Aleister Crowley.

This booklist is based upon the official lists issued by A.'.A.'. and published in Crowley's writings.* Additional listings are reproduced from V.H. Fra. N.'s unpublished *Catalogue and Key to the Technical Writings of Aleister Crowley*, the most comprehensive annotated survey to date. The *Catalogue and Key* is authoritative, and includes many *libri* that do not appear in the published lists.

---

* « A Syllabus of the Official Instructions of A.'.A.'. Hitherto Published,» *The Equinox* I(10) (London: 1913), with additional listings from the «Præmonstrance and Curriculum of A.'.A.'.,» *The Equinox* III(1) (Detroit: 1919) and *Magick in Theory and Practice* (Paris: Lecram, 1929), Appendix I.

Crowley explains the meaning of the A∴A∴ classification system as follows:

The publications of the A∴A∴ divide themselves into four classes.

Class «A» consists of books of which may be changed not so much as the style of a letter: that is, they represent the utterance of an Adept entirely beyond the criticism of even the Visible Head of the Organization.

Class «B» consists of books or essays which are the result of ordinary scholarship, enlightened and earnest.

Class «C» consists of matter which is to be regarded rather as suggestive than anything else.

Class «D» consists of the Official Rituals and Instructions.

Some publications are composite, and pertain to more than one class.*

A fifth class came into use *circa* 1919 E.V. (Class «E»), which Crowley applied to manifestos, broadsides, epistles and other public statements.

---

* Crowley, «Syllabus,» *op. cit.*, p. 43.

| | | | |
|---|---|---|---|
| | | B | *The Book of Thoth* |
| | | D | [A passage in *Liber CDXVIII*, 18th Æthyr.] |
| | | E | *The Equinox of the Gods* |
| | | E | *Genesis Libri AL* |
| I | 1 | A | *Liber B Vel Magi* |
| II | 2 | E | *The Message of the Master Therion* |
| III | 3 | D | *Liber Jugorum* |
| IV | 4 | | *Liber ABA* |
| V | 5 | D | *Liber V Vel Reguli* |
| VI | 6 | B | *Liber O Vel Manus et Sagittæ* |
| VII | 7 | A | *Liber Liberi Vel Lapis Lazuli, Adumbratio Kabbalæ Ægyptiorum* |
| VIII | 8 | D | *Liber VIII* |
| IX | 9 | B | *Liber E Vel Excercitiorum* |
| X | 10 | A | *Liber Porta Lucis* |
| XI | 11 | D | *Liber Nu* |
| XIII | 13 | D | *Graduum Montis Abiegni* |
| XV | 15 | | *O.T.O. Ecclesiæ Gnosticæ Catholicæ Canon Missæ* |
| XVI | 16 | B | *Liber Turris Vel Domus Dei* |
| XVII | 17 | D | *Liber IAO* |
| XXI | 21 | | *Khing Kang King* |
| XXIV | 24 | B | *De Nuptiis Secretis Deorum cum Hominibus* |
| XXV | 25 | D | *The Star Ruby* |
| XXVII | 27 | A | *Liber Trigrammaton* |
| XXVIII | 28 | D | *Liber Septem Regum Sanctorum, Ritual XXVIII, The Ceremony of the Seven Holy Kings* |
| XXVIII | 28 | | *Liber נצב Vel Νικη Sub Figurâ XXVIII, The Fountain of Hyacinth* |
| XXX | 30 | B | *Liber Libræ* |
| XXXI | 31 | A | *AL (Liber Legis), The Book of the Law* |
| XXXI | 31 | | *Liber XXXI* |
| XXXIII | 33 | C | *An Account of A∴A∴* |
| XXXVI | 36 | D | *The Star Sapphire* |
| XLI | 41 | C | *Thien Tao* |
| XLIV | 44 | D | *The Mass of the Phœnix* |
| XLVI | 46 | | *The Key of the Mysteries* |
| XLIX | 49 | | *Shi Yi Chien* |
| LI | 51 | | *The Lost Continent* |
| LII | 52 | | *Manifesto of the O.T.O.* |

# APPENDIX C
## Selected References

This appendix has two sections, a chronological list of principal editions of Class « A » material (including Classes « AB » and « A–B »), and a list of the principal commentaries to the Class « A » writings.

Many titles appear in both lists, *e.g.* volumes of commentaries that include the Class « A » text, uninterrupted by commentary, in a separate section.

An asterisk denotes the original source of each Class « A » text republished in the present edition.

Facsimile reprints are not included. For a general bibliography that includes reprints, see Parfitt and Drylie, *A Crowley Cross-Index* (Bath, U.K.: Zro, 1976).

## PRINCIPAL EDITIONS

Θελημα [THELEMA] (n.p., n.d.) [privately printed, 1909], 3 vols.
Vol. I includes *Liber LXV*\*, Vol. II is comprised of *Liber VII*\*, and Vol. III of *Libri XXVII*\*, *CCXX* and *DCCCXIII*\*. *Liber LXI* appeared in Class « A » in Vol. I, but was placed in Class « D » in a later publication.

THE EQUINOX I(3), London, 1910.
Includes *Liber CMLXIII* as a special supplement.

THE EQUINOX I(5), London, 1911.
Includes *Liber CDXVIII* as a special supplement.

THE EQUINOX I(6), London, 1911.
Includes *Libri X*\*, *XC*\*, *CLVI*\* and *CCCLXX*\*.

THE EQUINOX I(7), London, 1912.
Includes *Libri I*\*, *LXVI*\*, *CD*\*, and a photofacsimile of *Liber XXXI*. *Liber I* appeared in Class « B », but was placed in Class « A » in a later publication.

THE EQUINOX I(10), London, 1913.
Includes *Liber CCXX*.

THE EQUINOX III(1), Detroit, 1919.
Includes *Liber LXV*.

AL (LIBER LEGIS) SUB FIGURÂ XXXI (Tunis: privately printed, 1925).
A set of 65 photographic prints of the MS. of *Liber Legis*. A reprint of 65 printed sheets was issued the following year. This issue includes *The Comment* in Class « A ».

AN EXTENUATION OF THE BOOK OF THE LAW (Tunis: privately printed, 1926), 3 vols.
Includes *Libri XXVII* and *CCXX*, and *The Comment* in Class « A ».

MAGICK IN THEORY AND PRACTICE [LIBER IV, PART 3] (Paris: Lecram, 1929).
Includes *Libri I, CLVI* and *CCCLXX* in the appendices.

THE EQUINOX OF THE GODS (London: O.T.O., 1936).
Includes *Libri XXXI** and *CCXX*, and *The Comment** in Class « A ».

LIBER AL VEL LEGIS SUB FIGURÂ CCXX (London and Pasadena: O.T.O., 1938).
Includes *Liber CCXX* and *The Comment*.

LIBER XXX ÆRUM VEL SÆCULI SUB FIGURÂ CDXVIII . . .THE VISION AND THE VOICE (Barstow, Calif.: Thelema, 1952).
Includes *Liber CDXVIII*.

Θελημα [THELEMA] (Kitchener, Ont.: Alexander Watt, 1952).
Includes *Libri VII, XXVII, LXV, CCXX* and *DCCCXIII*.

THE HOLY BOOKS (Dallas: Sangreal, 1969).
Includes *Libri VII, LXV* and *DCCCXIII*.

THE MAGICAL RECORD OF THE BEAST 666 (Montréal, Next Step/93, and London: Duckworth, 1972).
Includes *Liber CCXX* as an appendix.

THE VISION AND THE VOICE (Dallas: Sangreal, 1972.)
Includes *Liber CDXVIII*.

MAGICK [LIBER IV, PARTS 1–3] (London: Routledge and Kegan Paul, 1973.)
Includes *Libri I, CLVI* and *CCCLXX* in the appendices.

AL (LIBER LEGIS) SUB FIGURÂ XXXI, THE BOOK OF THE LAW (San Francisco: Level, 1974).
Includes a variant typeset redaction of *Liber Legis* based upon one of several holograph manuscript copies of *Liber Legis* known to exist, but not the 1904 E.V. original. Technically, this edition is neither *Liber XXXI* nor *Liber CCXX*, except insofar as it includes a facsimile reprint of the latter.

GEMS FROM THE EQUINOX (St. Paul: Llewellyn, 1974).
Includes *Libri I, X, LXVI, XC, CLVI, CCXX, CCXXXI, CCCLXX, CD* and *CDXVIII*.

MAGICAL AND PHILOSOPHICAL COMMENTARIES ON THE BOOK OF THE LAW (Montréal: 93, 1974).
Includes a photoreproduction of *Liber XXXI* and *The Comment* in Class « A ».

THE COMMENTARIES OF AL (York Beach, ME: Weiser, 1975).
Includes a photoreproduction of *Liber XXXI* and *The Comment* in Class « A ».

The Law is for All (St. Paul: Llewellyn, 1975).
Includes *Libri CCXX* and *XXVII*, a photoreproduction of *Liber XXXI*, and *The Comment* in Class «A».

The Book of the Law (Montréal: 93, 1975).
Although subtitled *Liber AL Vel Legis Sub Figurâ CCXX*, this edition is actually an attempt to transcribe the MS., *Liber XXXI*, more exactly than did Crowley's edition—*Liber CCXX*. Reproduces *Liber XXXI* opposite the typeset redaction.

Liber AL Vel Legis Sub Figurâ CCXX (York Beach, ME: Weiser,1976).
Includes *Liber CCXX*\* and *The Comment* in Class «A», with the addition of a photore-production of *Liber XXXI*. In this reprint of the 1938 E.V. first edition, four typo-graphical errors were corrected by O.T.O.; these are listed on the copyright page of the 1976 E.V. edition.

The Equinox V(2) (Nashville: Thelema, 1979).
Includes *Liber CCXXXI*. This continuation of *The Equinox* series is considered apocryphal by many bibliographers.

The Book of the Law (Nashville: Troll, 1980)
A version of the text of *Liber Legis* that attempts to follow *Liber XXXI* more closely than does *Liber CCXX*. Technically, this edition is neither *Liber XXXI* nor *Liber CCXX*.

Sex and Religion (Nashville: Thelema, 1981).
Includes *Liber CDXV*.


# COMMENTARIES

Θελημα [Thelema] (n.p., n.d.) [privately printed, 1909], 3 vols.
Includes brief commentaries to *Libri VII, XXVII, LXV, CCXX* and *DCCCXIII*.

The Equinox I(6), London, 1911.
Includes a brief commentary to *Liber CCCLXX*.

The Equinox I(7), London, 1912.
Includes the Old Comment to *Liber Legis* and brief commentaries to *Libri CCXXXI* and *CD*.

An Extenuation of the Book of the Law (Tunis: privately printed, 1926), 3 vols.
Includes the Old and New Commentaries to *Liber Legis*, and a commentary to *Liber XXVII*.

The Equinox of the Gods (London: O.T.O., 1936).
Includes miscellaneous commentaries to *Liber Legis*.

Liber XXX Ærum Vel Sæculi Sub Figurâ CDXVIII . . . The Vision and the Voice (Barstow, Calif.: Thelema, 1952).
Includes the commentary to *Liber CDXVIII*.

Θελημα [Thelema] (Kitchener, Ont.: Alexander Watt, 1952).
Includes the *Preliminary Analysis of Liber LXV*.

THE VISION AND THE VOICE (Dallas: Sangreal, 1972.)

Includes an editorial abridgement of Crowley's commentary to *Liber CDXVIII*.

MAGICK [LIBER IV, PARTS 1–3] (London: Routledge and Kegan Paul, 1973.)

Includes a brief commentary to *Liber CCCLXX*.

MEZLA I(3), Buffalo, 1973.

Includes a commentary to *Liber LXVI*.

LIBER XXXI, by Frater Achad (San Francisco: Level, 1974).

*Liber XXXI*, written by Charles Stansfeld Jones, was accepted by Crowley as a legitimate commentary to *Liber Legis*; not to be confused with the MS. of *Liber Legis*, which bears the same title.

GEMS FROM THE EQUINOX (St. Paul: Llewellyn, 1974).

Includes brief commentaries to *Libri CCXXXI, CCCLXX* and *CD*.

MAGICAL AND PHILOSOPHICAL COMMENTARIES ON THE BOOK OF THE LAW (Montréal: 93, 1974).

Includes the Old Commentary to *Liber Legis*, an expanded version of the New Commentary, and «The Comment called ‹D›.» Also includes a commentary to *Liber XXVII*.

MEZLA I(4), Buffalo, 1974.

Includes a commentary to *Liber VII*.

SOTHIS I(3), St. Albans, 1974.

Includes *Liber XXXI*, Frater Achad's commentary to *Liber Legis*..

THE COMMENTARIES OF AL (York Beach, ME: Weiser, 1975).

Includes parts of the Old and New Commentaries to *Liber Legis*, and a commentary to *Liber XXVII*.

THE LAW IS FOR ALL (St. Paul: Llewellyn, 1975).

Includes the Old and New Commentaries to *Liber Legis*, and a commentary to *Liber XXVII*. Based upon *An Extenuation of the Book of the Law*.

MEZLA I(9), Buffalo, 1975.

Includes commentaries to *Liber CCCLXX* by Frater Achad and Crowley.

SOTHIS I(5), St. Albans, 1975.

Includes the *Preliminary Analysis of Liber LXV*.

IN THE CONTINUUM I(7-10), II(1) (Oroville, Calif.: College of Thelema, 1976-8)

Includes the *Preliminary Analysis of Liber LXV*.

THE EQUINOX V(2) (Nashville: Thelema, 1979).

Includes the *Preliminary Analysis of Liber LXV*.